Contents

Foreword
by the Living in Love and Faith Next Steps Group

The hopes, fears, discoveries, emotions, stories and prayers of many people fill these pages.

They represent the willingness of many thousands of people who call the Church of England their home to accept the invitation to learn together about how the Christian understanding of God relates to questions of identity, sexuality, relationships and marriage. They represent people's willingness to take risks as they open themselves to one another and to different convictions and perspectives about matters that are deeply personal. They represent much time and effort devoted to communicating thoughts and feelings by completing the questionnaire, taking part in a focus group or giving creative expression to their response.

As the group of bishops overseeing this remarkable churchwide engagement we want to express our own deep gratitude to every person represented in these pages. By means of this report, your views, prayers and heart cries will accompany the bishops as they attend to the Scriptures and seek to discern what the Spirit is saying to the Church of England at this time.

The Bishop of London, the Rt Revd and Rt Honourable Dame Sarah Mullally

The Bishop of Fulham, the Rt Revd Jonathan Baker

The Bishop of Grantham, the Rt Revd Dr Nicholas Chamberlain

The Bishop of Sherborne, the Rt Revd Karen Gorham

The Bishop of Ripon, the Rt Revd Dr Helen-Ann Hartley

The Bishop of Warrington, the Rt Revd Beverley Mason

The Bishop of Truro, the Rt Revd Philip Mounstephen

The Bishop of Bradwell, the Rt Revd Dr John Perumbalath

The Bishop of Maidstone, the Rt Revd Rod Thomas

Image (opposite): This painting was created by a person while they were taking part in a Living in Love and Faith focus group.

July 2022

4

Introduction

Gratitude and welcome

The gathered responses that are described in this booklet represent the willingness of thousands of people to respond to the invitation to engage with Living in Love and Faith (LLF) – often together with others. This has taken time, effort and remarkable courage: learning about and discussing topics of such deeply personal nature as identity, sexuality, relationships and marriage involves taking the risk of making oneself vulnerable.

It involved starting conversations that perhaps had never before taken place in church communities. It involved uncovering different perspectives, lived experiences and disagreements within church communities. Some of the responses in this booklet bear witness to the pain, anger, fear and sadness that engagement may have occasioned. However, as these pages show, the reward of encountering one another in the presence of Christ can be – and often has been – the joy of forming deeper relationships with one another and with God even across difference.

That is why this booklet begins and ends with gratitude: gratitude for the thousands of people who have given of themselves to the LLF process and without whose invaluable contributions the work of discernment and decision-making that follows the publication of this booklet would be vastly impoverished, if not impossible.

The risk and courage that engaging with Living in Love and Faith together with others requires is unevenly spread. It is far greater and more deeply personal for LGBTQ+ people. It is also challenging for people whose convictions seem to go against the grain of today's culture – both within the Church and outside it. The gratitude for these people especially is heartfelt and profound.

The aims of this report

Perhaps the best way to describe the first aim of this report, is to see it as a mirror. Its aim is to reflect back – as faithfully, impartially and accurately as possible – what those who have engaged with Living in Love and Faith have said by means of the questionnaire, the focus groups and creative submissions. The hope is that readers will hear their own voice in this report – as well as hearing and listening to the voices and views of others. Of course, not everyone has engaged with LLF and it is important – as far as possible – to hear these voices too. That is why this report also includes the voices of those who chose not to engage with LLF and explained why.

The second aim of the report is to ensure that the voices, perspectives and insights expressed through this churchwide engagement are listened to and heard by the bishops of the Church of England as they embark on the final stage of the journey in discerning a way forward for the Church of England during the autumn of 2022.

Over 6,400 people from all over the Church of England shared their learning and reflections about taking part in Living in Love and Faith by completing the LLF questionnaire. The responses to the questionnaire gave rise to many numbers and statistics, some of which are included in this report, and all of which can be found in a more detailed report that is available on the LLF website. Their aim is to describe the diversity of people who responded – in age, geographical location, and the words they have chosen to describe themselves and their relationships. Sometimes the numbers also provide evidence for the 'weight' of themes or perspectives among respondents.

The numbers do not offer the outcome of a poll or referendum on particular questions. Rather, the aim of this report is to offer a nuanced picture of the context in which the bishops' discernment and decision-making will take place.

The focus groups offered people an opportunity to reflect with others on their experience of taking part in the LLF Course. This interaction provided greater depth to the material that had been gathered through the questionnaire and provided a space for people with very different experiences and convictions to listen to one another and offer insights that might not otherwise have been heard.

Questions about identity, sexuality, relationships and marriage touch aspects of our lives that are deeply personal and relate to the very core of our faith and our shared identity in Christ. They challenge our intellect as well as our affections or emotions. They reach into aspects of our faith and being which are mysterious, and which are not always best expressed in words, propositions or arguments.

That is why this report also contains creative pieces that have been offered by individuals as expressions of their hopes and fears: not everyone finds words the best way to express themselves, and not all of what we want to say can be said in prose. Some of the creative pieces have been submitted through the LLF Learning Hub portal, others were created by individuals while they were taking part in one of the focus groups. The aim of these pieces – 'from the heart' – is to support and enrich the final phase of Living in Love and Faith as the Church moves from engaging and listening to discernment and decision-making.

To reflect back the voices and views from across the Church of England; to offer a nuanced and layered picture of churchwide hopes and fears; and to encourage receptivity to the Spirit in heart and mind: this report – like the LLF resources – does not aim to make any recommendations for a way forward for the Church. It is one of the resources which the bishops will draw upon to listen to what the Spirit may be saying to the Church of England – to understand how God may be shaping the Church today

The Living in Love and Faith journey

The Living in Love and Faith journey began in February 2017 when the Archbishops of Canterbury and York proposed that 'a large-scale teaching document around the subject of human sexuality' be commissioned. In their letter to members of General Synod they went on to say that 'in an episcopal church a principal responsibility of bishops is the teaching ministry of the church, and the guarding of the deposit of faith that we have all inherited. The teaching document must thus ultimately come from the bishops. However, all episcopal ministry must be exercised with all the people of God, lay and ordained, and thus our proposals will ensure a wide ranging and fully inclusive approach, both in subject matter and in those who work on it.'[1]

The four stages of the LLF process are shown in *Figure 1* and described below. The publication of this report marks the beginning of the final and fourth stage, namely discernment and decision-making.

Figure 1: The LLF Journey.

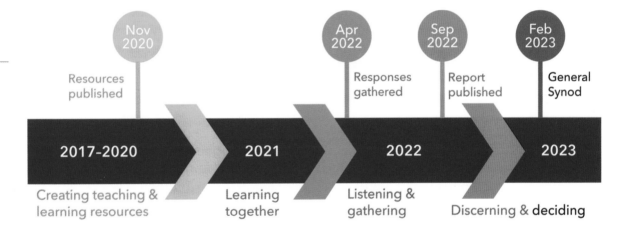

Creating teaching and learning resources

This was the starting point of the journey. It was a journey that would be led by the bishops and which the whole Church was invited to join. It was a journey that members of Synod were told would be 'a formidable undertaking. It will be costly, not only financially and in terms of people's time, but in terms of the process of exploring together matters that touch the very nature of our being. But nothing less will address the matter with the seriousness, the depth of wisdom and the diversity of possible approaches that should characterise authentic Christian exploration of the mystery of our humanity, of which our sexuality is an integral dimension.'

The 'teaching document' took the shape of a suite of resources under the banner, 'Living in Love and Faith: Christian teaching and learning about identity, sexuality, relationships and marriage'. They included a book, a course, podcasts, story films and an online library.

---

1   Letter to members of General Synod from the Archbishops of Canterbury and York, 17 February 2017. Available on https://www.churchofengland.org/sites/default/files/2017-11/abc-and-aby-joint-letter.pdf [Accessed 30 June 2022]

They were created collaboratively by a large multidisciplinary team of over forty people led by the Bishop of Coventry, Christopher Cocksworth. The resources were unanimously commended by the bishops for the whole Church to use to learn together and were published in November 2020. This represented the first milestone along the way.

Learning together

In addition to providing the whole church with rich resources for learning together, they contained clear signposts for the next stage of the journey: 'We, the Bishops of the Church of England, invite you to join us in using [the LLF resources] to learn together about how the Christian understanding of God relates to questions of identity, sexuality, relationships and marriage. [...] Our strong hope is that people and communities all around the country – everyone who looks to the Church of England as their spiritual home will engage with [the LLF resources] and, as far as possible, do this together with those who have different perspectives and lived experiences.'[2]

Within a week of their publication, over 280 people in Exeter Diocese joined an online 'taster day' to find out more about the LLF resources and how to engage with them. By the end of another twelve months, almost six thousand people engaged in further taster sessions across most dioceses. Living in Love and Faith Advocates were appointed in every diocese to help animate, encourage and support engagement as widely as possible across the Church. Training for facilitators was provided and gradually, groups started to form to study the course. Many engaged online as dictated by COVID-19 lockdown restrictions. Others preferred to wait until it was possible to engage in person. It was decided, therefore, to extend the timeframe for feeding back – while emphasising the value of continuing to take part after the window for responding had closed.

Listening and gathering

As this second stage of churchwide engagement got underway – led by the Next Steps Group of Bishops chaired by the Bishop of London, Sarah Mullally – preparations were already being made for the third stage of the journey. This too, was spelled out in the LLF resources: the LLF Course assured participants that their 'experiences, learning and discernment will be gathered, listened to and reflected on by the bishops together with members of General Synod as they discern the way forward for the Church of England regarding questions of identity, sexuality, relationships and marriage.'

In order for this listening to take place, ways had to be found for gathering what was emerging from this churchwide engagement. It was agreed to offer people three ways of sharing their learning, reflections and experience of engaging with LLF. These were by completing the LLF questionnaire, joining a focus group and offering a creative response. These – and the other ways in which people chose to respond – are described in more detail below. The window for sending in responses closed at the end of April 2022 – over a year later than originally planned.

It was important for people to be able to respond in ways that were accessible, holistic and open-ended. This was not simply an exercise in gauging the 'majority mind' of the Church about particular questions – as important and informative as that is – it was and is about listening to what the Spirit is saying to the Church today. It is about seeking the mind of Christ together. This means being open to unanticipated reflections from

---

2   The LLF Book (*Living in Love and Faith: Christian teaching and learning about identity, sexuality, relationships and marriage*, Church House Publishing, London: 2020) page 420.

surprising sources. It means listening to the voices that are less often heard in the cacophony that disagreement so easily creates.

Discerning and deciding

The publication of this report – and the more detailed version on the LLF website – signals the beginning of the final stage of the LLF journey: discernment leading to decision-making about a way forward for the Church of England in relation to questions about identity, sexuality, relationships and marriage.

This part of the journey is still ahead of us: it will be led by the bishops of the Church of England who will meet over three residential gatherings in September, October/November and December 2022. For one day in each of these gatherings, the bishops will be accompanied by members of the LLF Reference Group, who embody diverse lived experiences and convictions, and are a mix of lay and ordained people. Their role will be to enrich the bishops' discussions by offering perspectives from outside the episcopal arena; to ensure that the insights and sensibilities of diverse lived experiences and convictions are embedded in the discernment process; and to act as a diverse sounding board for any conclusions, recommendations or plans.

With this publication in their hands, together with the LLF resources, the Bible, and the tradition of the Church enshrined in its formularies – as well as their own life experience and that of those known to them – the bishops will begin the process of discernment. They do so accompanied by the reflections, experiences, longings and prayers of the thousands of people from across the Church whose voices this report has tried to capture. They do so with the Archbishops' promise ringing in their ears, 'that this process would reflect a *radical new Christian inclusion, … founded in scripture, in reason, in tradition, in theology and the Christian faith as the Church of England has received it.*"' Above all, they do so in the power of the Holy Spirit, committing themselves to prayer and an openness to one another and to God.

At the end of this period of discernment the bishops will offer their reflections that will include a clear sense of direction about the way forward for the Church regarding matters of identity, sexuality, relationships and marriage – and perhaps other matters that have arisen during the LLF process and that the Church needs to attend to. The bishops' reflections will be brought to the February 2023 sessions of General Synod for decision-making.

How responses were heard and gathered

This section describes the sources of data which this report draws upon. Much more detail about the methodologies used, the questions asked, and the data gathered can be found on the LLF website (www.churchofengland.org/LLF) in the report, 'Listening with Love and Faith: Gathered responses in detail'.

The LLF questionnaire

A questionnaire was used to enable as many people as possible to share their thoughts and experiences. The questionnaire was designed and managed by Brendan Research, in collaboration with the diocesan LLF Advocates and the LLF Next Steps Group. It was structured on the basis that the vast majority of people who engaged with Living in Love and Faith did so by taking part in the LLF Course together with others.

6,448 people responded using the questionnaire, representing a high response rate, especially for a questionnaire that involved considerable time, thought and effort to complete. The questionnaire included sections on where respondents lived, their age group, and the words they used to describe themselves, to monitor the diversity of respondents across the Church. It included open-ended questions to allow people to respond as freely and fully as possible, thereby capturing unanticipated responses about what was important to the respondent.

Questions included what respondents had learned from the course, whether the aims of the LLF Course had been met, how they experienced the course, and what difference engaging with both the course and with others had made. The questionnaire asked what difference respondents hoped that engaging with the course will make for their local church and for the Church nationally. While the qualitative analysis of responses to these questions identifies popular answers and prominent themes, more importantly it bears out the diversity of views that exist and their complex interactions.

The questionnaire was linked from the LLF website[3] and the LLF Learning Hub[4], and information about it was disseminated in a variety of ways across dioceses. The questionnaire was open between 30 March 2021 and 30 April 2022. Most people completed the questionnaire online. However, the questionnaire was available offline and could be completed electronically and emailed, or printed and completed by hand. These were added to the online system and analysed with the others.

Privacy and data protection were of utmost importance and an introductory section detailed the uses to which the data would be put, and the safeguards in place. All the responses were read by the analysis team to ensure any safeguarding issues were passed on. The qualitative data was processed using qualitative data analysis software. Responses to the questions were sorted into themes or 'codes' that were continually adapted to capture themes as they emerged and became clearer. This is an iterative process enabling the researchers to become very familiar with the content of the questionnaires and to integrate the statistical and textual elements of the data and understand how they related to each other.

Focus groups

One of the questions in the questionnaire invited respondents to offer to be part of a focus group. All individuals who had indicated a willingness to take part by the end of November 2021 were invited to participate in an online or onsite focus group. Those who replied to the invitation were subsequently informed of the details of the online and onsite groups. All potential participants who could attend and had selected a group were contacted and invited to participate. The focus groups were organised and facilitated by the Church Army Research Unit.

Four online groups were held between December 2021 and January 2022. Five in-person groups were held in different parts of the country – northeast, northwest, east and southwest – between December 2021 and March 2022. The number of participants in a group ranged from 5 to 12. The total number of participants was 112 and represented diversity in age as well as in relation to sexuality, gender and relationship status.

---

3   https://www.churchofengland.org/resources/living-love-and-faith
4   https://llf.churchofengland.org

The groups used both creative and discussion elements. They were 'anonymous' in that participants' personal characteristics were not known before attending a focus group. None of the focus groups were made aware of the facilitators' personal views and there were always at least two facilitators, both of whom acted as facilitators and note-takers.

As part of the focus groups, participants were invited to create an artistic piece, providing an additional opportunity for participants to share their thoughts and feelings. The majority of participants, both in the online and onsite focus groups, took part in this element, providing a rich array of creative and prayerful expressions of their engagement with the LLF process. Many of these responses are reproduced in this report. Some are accompanied by explanatory captions written by the person who created the artwork.

The discussion element offered all participants the opportunity to express themselves freely and with active consent, within the 'commitments' set out in the LLF Course. The exact questions that were used varied from group to group, as participants' responses and the conversations took different directions. Here are some examples of questions that were used:

What do you remember about how you felt at the start of the course?

What surprised you as you did the course?

How have your views changed or developed during the course?

How have you responded to people whose views are very different from your own?

How has your understanding of the church as a community changed?

Has your understanding of God developed in any way?

Are there people who have felt excluded from the church?

What kind of church do you think God wants?

What would you like to say to the church?

Creative responses – and an art installation

People who engaged with LLF were also invited to send in a creative response through the LLF Hub. This gave participants an opportunity to express themselves in a way that reflected the innate creativity of human beings who bear the image of the creator God. It enabled people to convey the LLF experience in a way that is affective and effective, recognising that the rich diversity of people and their lives of faith and love within the Church of England is most fully explored and expressed not just in words and numbers but in conversations, relationships, images, artwork, music and stories.

The creative responses were gathered and managed by ASD Arts and Education Ltd. Many creative responses were pieces of visual art: sketches, paintings, posters, sculptures, craftwork. Others were in written form – poems, prayers, narrative text. Groups were also invited to send in photos, videos or audio recordings of reflections from their group. Two of these were songs written and composed in response to LLF. A total of 58 creative responses were received, in addition to videos of groups' and individuals' feedback. Images of some of the creative responses can be found in this report. All of them can be found online and were mounted as an audiovisual installation at the July 2022 sessions of General Synod for members to engage with.

The report also contains close-up images of an art installation that was commissioned for and inspired by LLF and has been on display at York Minster between July and September 2022. Entitled, 'Faith and Fracture', the sculpture comprises thousands of pieces of weathered glass threaded on sixteen strands of wire suspended over the York Minster transept. Created by Alice Walker and David Ferrier, the sculpture was accompanied by an evocative soundscape composed by Matt Eaton. Like the thousands of pieces of glass that make up the sculpture, it gave visual impact to the many thousands of people across the country who responded to the invitation to learn together about human identity, sexuality, relationships and marriage. As a piece of public art, it invited visitors to reflect on what faith might have to say to a world of conflict, disagreement and fracture. A virtual tour of the sculpture with soundscape can be found on the LLF website.

'Faith and Fracture' art installation at York Minster.

Independent submissions

At the start of the engagement and listening process, it was envisaged that analysis of the completed questionnaires, together with the feedback from focus groups and an invitation to respond creatively, would be sufficient to summarise the breadth and depth of responses from the LLF process. However, guidance on submitting feedback was not as clear and consistent as it should have been. By the time the window for responding had closed, therefore, over 250 responses had been received from individuals and churches that were not in the form of a completed questionnaire or a creative response. About one fifth of these were from groups or individuals who had chosen not to engage with LLF. Others had not wished to use the questionnaire or wanted to supplement the questionnaire with a fuller response.

All these responses were read and received by the LLF Coordinator and were analysed by the Brendan Research team as described in the 'Listening with Love and Faith: Gathered responses in detail'. The responses were informative of the complexity of the questions raised as well as offering insight into the viewpoints of those that are underrepresented in survey and focus group data: churches in more deprived areas and those younger than the average age of questionnaire respondents.

In this report, these responses are illustrated by means of a selection of short 'stories' drawing on these independently submitted pieces that had been received from both churches and individuals. More of these 'stories' can be found in the detailed report. They are intended to be illustrative rather than representative and, as such, hopefully offer insights into the variety, breadth and complexity of views and feelings that engaging – or not – with LLF have prompted.

How responses are presented

The remainder of this report seeks to offer a faithful, accurate and evidenced account of what has been seen and heard through the questionnaires, the focus groups, the creative responses and independent submissions. Beginning with an analysis of the thousands of people who shared their experience of engaging with LLF, the remainder of the booklet reflects some of the headings under which people's responses were most readily described: learning, relating, being church, and moving forward.

In order to stay as true as possible to people's own voices, short summary statements are 'evidenced' by a sample of direct quotes taken from questionnaires or from focus group contributions. These are interspersed with creative responses from the focus groups and pieces submitted via the LLF Hub. Much more detail can be found in the 'Listening with Love and Faith: Gathered responses in detail' report on the LLF website.

Each chapter ends with a 'story' that is drawn anonymously from submissions that were sent in 'independently', usually via the LLF website. Some will be from individuals or churches who engaged with LLF, and some from those who did not.

The Conclusion offers a brief account of the final stage of the LLF journey: discernment and decision-making.

Taking part

Who took part?

6,448 people from all over the Church of England shared their learning and reflections about taking part in Living in Love and Faith by completed the LLF questionnaire. This represents the most extensive churchwide survey carried out by the Church of England to date. While a very encouraging response, the actual number of people who engaged with LLF is considerably greater, as this only represents those who chose to respond using the questionnaire.

LLF at St Christopher's Church, Hinchley Wood.

In this section we describe some aspects of the diversity of the people who took part in LLF and responded through the questionnaire and focus groups. Much more detailed analysis can be found in 'Listening with Love and Faith: Responses in detail'.

Geography

People responded from all areas of England and all Church of England dioceses. Responses were received from major cities to small villages and hamlets, and from very deprived areas to areas with little deprivation. Compared with England as a whole, there were fewer responses from more deprived areas, and more responses from rural areas than we would expect.

Age

People of all ages took part, but few responses came from those who said they were 24 or under. 83% of responses came from people aged 45 or over.

Figure 2:
Age of
respondents.

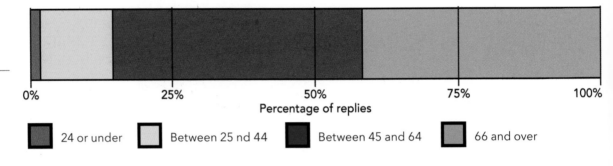

Percentage of replies

- 24 or under
- Between 25 nd 44
- Between 45 and 64
- 66 and over

Gender

Participants were invited to select one or more 'identifying words' to describe themselves. In relation to gender, respondents could choose 'female', 'intersex', 'male', 'gender-fluid' and/or 'non-binary'. All options could be selected in combination with others. *Figure 3* gives details of numbers.

Figure 3:
Identifying
words used by
respondents
to describe
themselves.

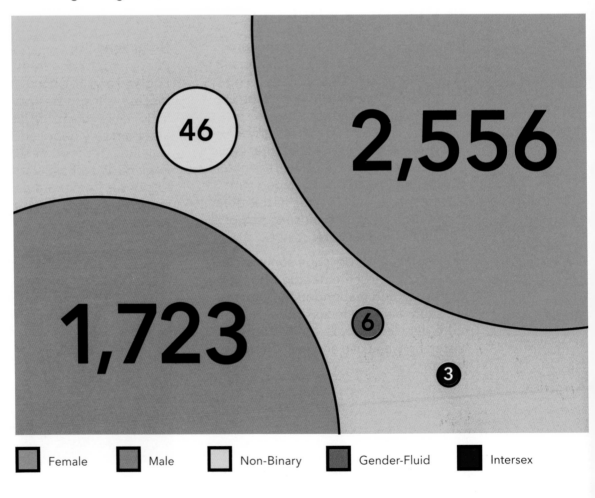

- Female
- Male
- Non-Binary
- Gender-Fluid
- Intersex

The identifiers, 'transgender' and 'cisgender' were also offered as options. Only a relatively small proportion of people chose to use the identifier, 'cisgender'.

Figure 4: People who chose to describe themselves as cisgender or transgender.

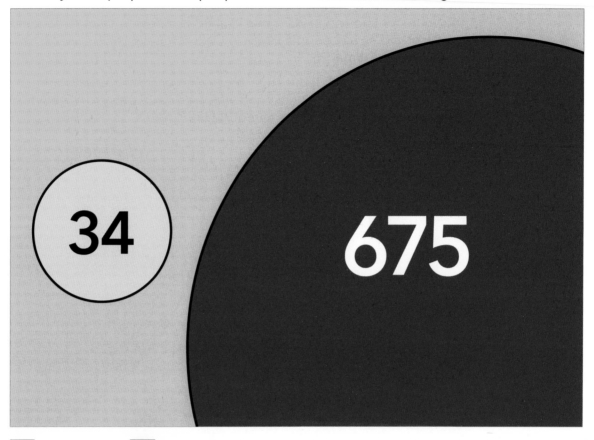

34 675

☐ Transgender ■ Cisgender

LLF at Chelmsford.

Sexuality

89% (4,423 people) of those who indicated a response in this section described themselves as heterosexual. The UK Office for National Statistics (ONS) estimates that the figure for England in 2020 was 94.4%.[5] The next most common responses were gay|lesbian (7%; 347 people | 1.8% in ONS estimates) and bisexual (3.5%; 175 people |1.2% in ONS estimates).

Write-in responses of demisexual (those who only feel sexually attracted to someone when they have an emotional bond with them) and pansexual (those who are attracted to all genders) were included as categories in *Figure 5*.

Figure 5: Identifying words used by respondents to describe their sexuality.

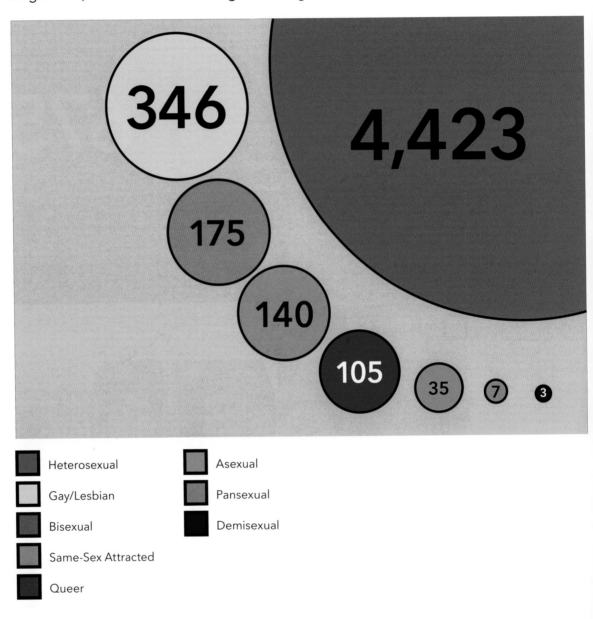

Heterosexual

Gay/Lesbian

Bisexual

Same-Sex Attracted

Queer

Asexual

Pansexual

Demisexual

5   Sexual Orientation, UK https://www.ons.gov.uk/peoplepopulationandcommunity/culturalidentity/sexuality/bulletins/sexualidentityuk/2020 [Accessed 25 May 2022]

Relationship

Over half (61%; 3,304 people) of respondents described themselves as married to someone of the opposite sex. 12% (661 people) described themselves as single, and 3% (160 people) described themselves as in a same-sex marriage. A substantial number of people wrote in that they were a widow or widower (3.5%; 189 people) or divorced or separated (2.3%; 124 people). Ten people described themselves as remarried. These categories may refer to former opposite-sex or same-sex marriages. In addition, three people said that they had vowed celibacy, some within a community. A significant number (3.3%; 178 people) described themselves as co-habiting.

Figure 6: Words used by respondents to describe their relationships.

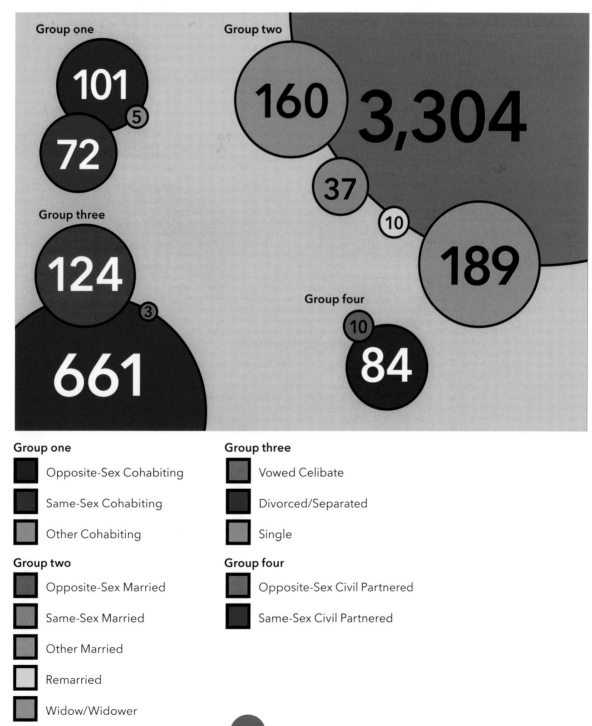

Group one
- ⬛ Opposite-Sex Cohabiting
- ⬛ Same-Sex Cohabiting
- ⬜ Other Cohabiting

Group two
- ⬛ Opposite-Sex Married
- ⬜ Same-Sex Married
- ⬜ Other Married
- ⬜ Remarried
- ⬜ Widow/Widower

Group three
- ⬛ Vowed Celibate
- ⬛ Divorced/Separated
- ⬜ Single

Group four
- ⬜ Opposite-Sex Civil Partnered
- ⬛ Same-Sex Civil Partnered

Reflections

In choosing which words to use to describe themselves, participants were offered the opportunity to add a note to their selection. For some people, this gave them the freedom to describe themselves in a more nuanced way:

> "Fluid, ever changing; emotionally more lesbian, sexually more heterosexual."

> "Some aspects of my persona are not stereotypically male."

Some people noted that the reason they were participating was to better understand family members:

> "My daughter identifies as bisexual, so I have her in mind as I take this course."

> "Heterosexual parent of a gay, trans adult child."

> "Son of a same-sex attracted man, who decided to live in accordance with church teaching, for which I am thankful."

A painting created in response to engaging with LLF entitled, 'Knit Together'.

in our mother's womb

Knitted in our mother's wombs

Jan

Our deepest identity is to be found in Christ

God given diversity, each of us is unique

All created by God.

Who didn't take part?

It is not possible to know exactly how many people took part in LLF. It is likely that far more did than is represented by the number of questionnaires completed. Several questionnaire respondents emphasised that the impact of LLF depends on the degree of engagement with the course. It was highlighted that church leaders' decisions to promote the course, and the inclusion of people with diverse viewpoints, will be deciding factors in whether and how LLF shapes a way forward for the Church of England.

"

For it to make any difference more people need to do the course."

"Very little [impact] as apart from the clergy I am not aware of any others taking the course."

"Don't think it will make a difference as perhaps the curious to learn signed up for the course, whilst others declined."

Some members of the GLU (God Loves U) Youth Group from St Mary's Church Partington and their leaders, who took part in LLF.

Although all the focus group participants had been part of an LLF Course group, they offered thoughts about the voices that were missing and why others might not have got involved:

"People at one end or the other didn't want to join in. I would've liked more diversity but it's difficult and not everybody wants to be open and vulnerable."

"It was noticeable who was not engaging with the course… there was a fear that if people did engage, they would somehow be endorsing something or going in a direction they did not want to go."

"A lot of people aren't interested – and asked why we are still talking about this – they thought it was sorted 10 to 15 years ago."

"After doing the course, I attended deanery synod and saw that there were a lot of people who had already made up their minds about the course without having attended it. One was promoting an alternative."

"The worst part was how some parts of the Church denigrated the course or refused to take part."

A minority of participants stated that others simply did not know about the LLF Course:

"My parish doesn't even know this course exists, despite my best efforts."

LLF at Wolverton.

A number of independent submissions from churches which had chosen not to take part in LLF offered insights into why they had reached this decision. The following comments are representative of a fairly equal spread of views.

"The course would not prove useful in our context because it would inevitably lead to the questioning of the lives, loves and relationships of those in the congregation who are LGBTQI, would be pastorally inappropriate and damaging."

"[…] it has been hard for our people to engage with a process that seems to be asking them to put their identity into dialogue with another person's opinion. [...] While we want to find a way for the body of Christ to stay together, our people speak of feeling assaulted and bruised when they are asked to allow their identity to become a subject of others' rejection and condemnation. The risks on the two sides of the argument do not seem commensurate."

"However, having read the book and looked over some of the resources it seems there is a lack of proper, detailed engagement with Scripture. […] Whilst Scripture is referenced as 'our final authority' it does not seem to be treated as such. We feel LLF raises lots of good questions but does little to further the discussion and debate in answering them."

"most working class people have a lot going on in their lives with work, family and church responsibilities that taking a large chunk of time out of several weekends is a huge commitment and not practical for most."

"While the LLF process describes the disagreements it makes no attempt to seek to resolve them or provide any basis for authority for discerning between them. The result is that the resources raise questions but do not provide any form of answer. At best this creates uncertainty, at worst it creates the perception of relativism, that every individual can opt for the position with which they most closely identify. This is not an approach consistent with belief in a God who has authority over our lives and who has given us his word as a lamp for our feet. It is this concern that meant that the church leadership were unable to commend the course to our church family. It feels to us that there was an expectation that through the resources some 'new truth' on the key issues may emerge, upon which the church would somehow 'decide'."

A number of churches and individuals also made reference to the timing of LLF and the difficulty of engaging because of the pressures of COVID-19 on the life and ministry of the church.

What did people say about taking part?

Participants' overall experience of the LLF Course

In gathering the responses of people who took part in the LLF Course, it was important to listen to participants' evaluation of the course, as this is likely to affect the significance and quality of answers to the more in-depth questions about learning, relating, being church and discerning a way forward. Participants were asked, therefore, to describe their overall experience of the LLF Course by placing a slider between 'terrible' (0) and 'wonderful' (100).

Figure 7 shows the responses received. Most people found the course to be a positive experience, with scores just under 75 out of 100. There is a plateau between 25 and 37, representing a group of people who found the experience of the course less helpful. The average (mean) score was 59 – overall, a fairly positive response.

Three-quarters (73%) of respondents said that they would recommend the course to a friend. We might expect that some people who did not like the course would not bother to complete a feedback response, but this is a high number for such an exercise.

A popular reason for recommending the course to others, for example, was its high quality and for the way it stimulated discussion and provoked thought and reflection. The course was described as "balanced and informative" and "carried out with love and humility". The story films received particularly high praise across several of the survey questions. People appreciated having "real life" examples to think with and discuss. A number noted the helpful mix of components: Bible study, short films and discussion questions. The Pastoral Principles were seen as an "excellent foundation" for discussion.

Figure 7: Overall experience of the LLF Course.

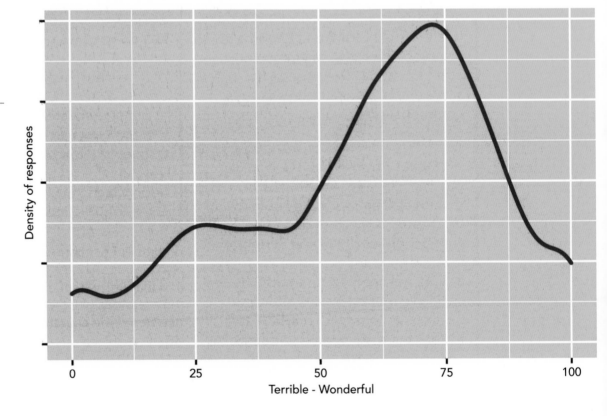

Density of responses

Terrible - Wonderful

0   25   50   75   100

Others, however, described the course using words such as: dense, confusing, wordy, lacked clarity, vague, woolly, superficial, flimsy, bland, anodyne, patronising. Some critiqued the discussion questions as not helpful, superficial and failing to address the urgency and depth of the subject matter.

A response created while taking part in a focus group:
I drew a tube of oil paint - squeezing a lot of words out about the experience of the course. I chose oil paint because it's hard to come off. Some of the words are... story, positive, division, voice, mistrust.

A response created while taking part in a focus group:
I drew a scale or see-saw. The positives of the course on the one side outweighed the negative on the other side. Positives include breadth and pastoral principles. Negative was partly local difficulties and partly lack of depth.

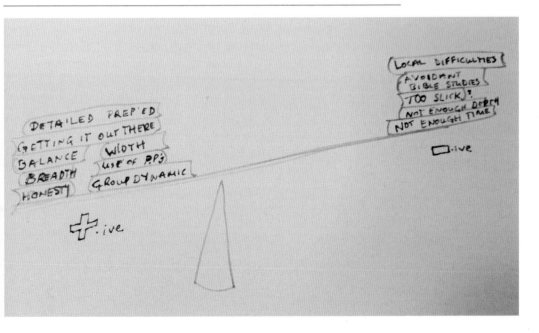

Leaders' overall experience of the LLF Course

A number of the respondents commented on the way in which the experience of the course was affected by the course leaders. Part of the questionnaire was directed towards course leaders to explore their experience of leading their group. *Figure 8* shows that people found the experience of leading the LLF Course positive with the mean score being 70 and the median 74 out of 100.

> "Pleased to be part of something the church has avoided for far too long. Challenged to keep conversations from being divisive or unhelpful. Satisfied to have run the course to completion. Accepting that we don't all have the same opinions but are willing to listen to each other."

> "I was hesitant at first, but consider the issues addressed in the course to be so important that I was prepared to take the plunge."

> **" It was really exciting, a word I would rarely use in this context, and also helped me work through my own views and prejudices."**

The LLF Course group materials were reported to be very helpful indeed with 87% of leaders finding them to be usually or always helping the group to engage with the topics.

> "It was a real privilege – and very easy, given the user-friendly nature of the material."

> "the videos really helped to frame discussion and to keep some personal distance for me as leader."

Figure 8: Overall experience of leading the LLF Course.

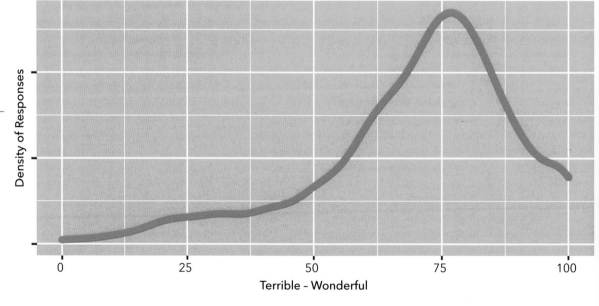

Density of Responses

Terrible - Wonderful

0   25   50   75   100

Some expressed that preparation could be time-consuming, and it was challenging to represent different views. For a minority of participants, the experience of facilitating a group had a personal cost.

> **"**
>
> *I found it difficult to remain impartial because we're talking about real people, real problems."*

"I held back as a facilitator to make sure the conservative voices in the room felt safe enough to speak."

Leaders who received training before the course were grateful for it and some who did not, said it would have been helpful.

Perceptions about the aim of the course

Several respondents commented that the material was "biased", "selective", "one sided". The course was identified as having an underlying "agenda". While some stated that the course assumes the conservative position to be "normative", others felt that the course was designed to change the Church of England's teaching on sex and relationships, sometimes portraying traditional/conservative Christians as "ignorant".

"It is carefully selected and does not cover human sexuality in a balanced way."

"At times it felt there was a bias towards 'traditionalism'."

"I felt that the course had quite a strong agenda. I happen to be quite aligned with it, but I felt a bit sorry for people with different opinions."

"There seems to me to be a very clear agenda behind the course and that is that of a determination to change the church's – and God's – teaching on relationships and sex."

"I suspected there was a hidden agenda which made me feel angry."

This theme was reflected in the focus groups: some participants were angry and frustrated because they thought that there was an unacknowledged standpoint being advocated through the material and the structure of the course. It is interesting to note that what the hidden agenda or unacknowledged standpoint was perceived to be varied depending on participants' own theology or personal convictions.

How varied were the groups?

One of the aims of LLF was to encourage people to learn together across different convictions and lived experiences, listening well to one another with an openness to understand and learn. The questionnaire asked how varied were the groups in which respondents took part. *Figure 9* shows that the groups were roughly equally split between being quite varied, and quite similar – there are two major "bumps" in the data.

A number of respondents who had taken part in a group with little diversity recognised that this impoverished their engagement with the course and with each other.

Some of the focus group discussions raised the involvement of both ordained and lay people as an important factor in group composition, with clergy often taking on the role of group leader or facilitator. Some groups were exclusively clergy, and it was suggested by one participant this may have allowed some clergy to be more open in their personal views.

"As clergy, we spoke very well to each other. We all learned things. It would have been massively different if lay people had been present."

Figure 9: Variety within the groups.

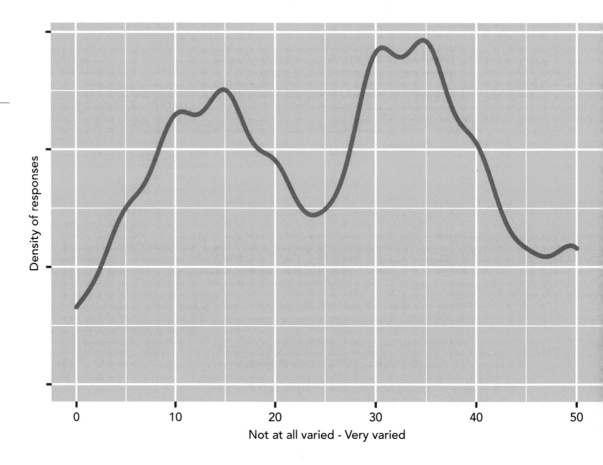

Density of responses

0   10   20   30   40   50

Not at all varied - Very varied

A few participants commented that when clergy met with lay people they were perhaps holding back for the sake of the unity in their church or parish context. Others thought that the laity were more able to express stronger or personal views.

> "One of the frustrations I have is that no clergy person is prepared to say actually what they believe, because we're so terrified of upsetting the laity."

> "The laity are a long way ahead of where the clergy are in many cases."

> "I do wonder whether clergy have been the bottle stop out of fear of what we might release ... whether [that] is [the] Holy Spirit doing something in our church, with lay people standing up."

A response created while taking part in a focus group with the following commentary: "Jass (a pseudonym) - Red is for anger. I knew 'I just had to have red'. The purple spots and clapperboard pictures refer to the sessions - every session gave us an opportunity to share about our lives - a scene from our lives ... but at the end of the course we all said, 'what was that?' Why did we feel an underlying narrative that wasn't ours? We had to reclaim quite a lot of ground. This was not an even playing field. God was with me. Not a statistic. Everybody hurts."

Stories about
taking part:

'So that made five reasons against participating, and three in favour. Nevertheless, I went along, and am glad that I did.'

'I attended the Living in Love and Faith Course in [early] 2022. I am a father [...] a layman, and an out gay man in a relationship. This is simply my entirely personal experience of the programme. I very nearly didn't attend. To prepare myself, I read through the course booklet and paid attention to public comment on a number of Christian LGBT social media accounts that I follow. I wondered whether or not to bother with the course and weighed up the factors, making a list of pros and cons.

Against going:

I was sceptical that any amount of listening to each other was likely to produce agreement, let alone change and justice.

I thought the course booklet was weak on reasons why we have to stop using the Bible to proof-text moral condemnations of LGBT people. Some more direct teaching on that would have been helpful.

The course booklet and other materials dodged the problem of the C of E's status as an established church, which cannot change its position on equal marriage without Parliament's permission.

Wider issues such as misogyny, sexual puritanism and prurience were also avoided.

Would I just be wasting my time and perhaps exposing myself to bible-bashers?

In favour of going:

The course booklet acknowledged the levels of fear that exist in addressing the church's divisions about sexuality.

The materials made a genuine attempt to be even-handed.

There was also acknowledgement of hypocrisy in the church. Generally I felt that this level of honesty should be credited.

So that made five reasons against participating, and three in favour. Nevertheless, I went along, and am glad that I did.'

Gay, cisgender male, over 65 years

'...looking at this material has helped me to solidify my view that the Bible has very clear, helpful, compassionate and relevant teaching on marriage and singleness, sexuality and gender.'

'I think that looking at this material has helped me to solidify my view that the Bible has very clear, helpful, compassionate and relevant teaching on marriage and singleness, sexuality and gender. It has helped me to see that God's good design for people (for their flourishing and his glory) is that marriage is for one man and one woman, that sexuality (whether married or single) is designed to show God's glory and that gender is a good gift given to us by God. This is good news! It's also helped me to think about how we must be a compassionate and welcoming safe space for everyone.'

Heterosexual, female, single, 45–64 years

'From this engagement, the majority recognised that 'compassion and love should always be chosen over fear and judgmentalism.'

A church in a parish 'characterised by financial, educational and health poverty' shared their experience of engaging with the LLF material. Describing themselves as 'multi-ethnic, multi-lingual, multi-generational and multi-ability', they introduced themselves as having 'a spirit of openness to all'.

The vicar, with backing from the PCC, began with 'a preaching series on the pastoral principles'. As a result, some congregation members commented that they could now 'voice their support' for change. Those who were unsure about same-sex marriage 'remained challenged' but felt it might be 'a generational issue for them'.

'A couple of months later a listening exercise was offered on a Saturday morning.' Five of the film resources were played to represent 'different types of story'. After each one, a time of silence was kept and everyone present was invited to 'share one single word as a response'. This they described as three-way listening – listening to the experience of those in the films, to God and to one another.

To conclude, they shared their responses to the questions: 'What is the Spirit saying to the church?' and 'What does the church want to say in response to the consultation?' From this engagement, the majority recognised that 'compassion and love should always be chosen over fear and judgmentalism'.

Looking ahead, their existing spirit of welcome will 'now more naturally extend towards those whose experiences of sexuality and gender are different to our own'. The majority expressed a wish to 'offer God's blessing on same-sex relationships including marriage', but as a church they did not feel it was right to take a 'vote' at this stage because they 'seek to move together as a community and try not to bring things to a division on any issue'.

Learning

How much did participants learn?

One of the aims of Living in Love and Faith is to encourage the whole church to engage in deeper learning about human identity, sexuality, relationships and marriage in the context of the Christian faith. It was important, therefore, to find out whether such learning had taken place.

How familiar was the material to participants?

The questionnaire first asked participants how new the material was to them, on a scale of 0 - very familiar, to 100 - very new.

Figure 10 shows the responses obtained for each of the five sessions of the LLF Course:

1. What does it mean to learn together as followers of Jesus Christ?

2. How does our identity in Christ relate to sex and gender?

3. What kinds of relationships does God call us to?

4. Where do our bodies and sex fit in to all of this?

5. How do diversity and difference affect our life together as a church?

The responses, like those concerned with group variety, have two "bumps" – one around the 25 mark, and another around the 60 point. This means that for some people, the material was not very new – they'd met it before, while for others, they were meeting new material.

Session 1, on Learning Together, contained the most familiar material for participants – its aqua-coloured curve is distinctively high on the left of *Figure 10* – followed by the pink curve for Session 3, Relationships. The remaining sessions had similar average responses, with roughly equal curves.

*Figure 10:
Novelty of the
material in the
LLF Course.*

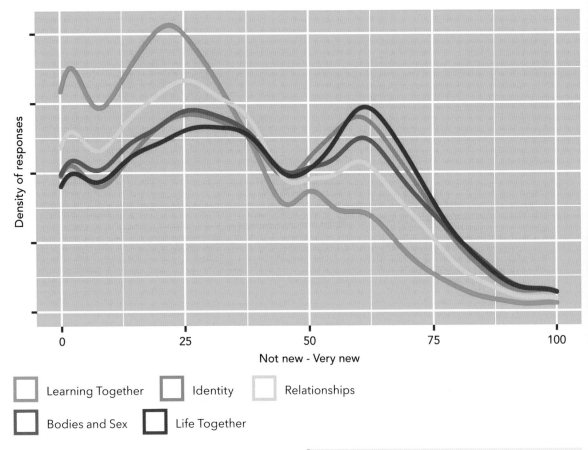

Density of responses

Not new - Very new

☐ Learning Together   ☐ Identity   ☐ Relationships

☐ Bodies and Sex   ☐ Life Together

Some of the survey respondents told us that that the course made little difference to them because they were already familiar with the material. While a few of those respondents were frustrated by this, a larger number still felt the course was worthwhile and were glad their church was engaging with the material.

"I actually found it slightly annoying. Perhaps this is because I have done some reading and thinking through these issues for myself I found it a bit patronising."

"It was interesting to hear different view points, but I don't think I learned much that I didn't already know."

"I had already thought and read a lot on LGBTQI inclusion before the course, so probably it has not made a big difference, but it was good that some of my church engaged in it."

Did learning result in deeper understanding?

The LLF Course aimed to deepen understanding of topics relating to identity, sexuality, relationships and marriage, in the following areas:

• teaching from the Bible;

• the inherited teaching of the Church;

• emerging Christian views on these topics; and

• understanding different views and encountering different experiences.

Questionnaire respondents were asked if their understanding had been deepened in these areas, using a sliding scale from 0 to 100, where 100 indicates the strongest agreement, and 0 the strongest disagreement.

The results – shown in *Figure 11* – indicate that, on average, most people's engagement with LLF brought about deeper understanding about all four areas. The highest scores related to a greater awareness 'of the complexities of identity, sexuality, relationships and marriage' (66), and an ability 'to relate more compassionately and respectfully to people with different views from mine' (64).

There is plenty of evidence from the focus groups that learning did take place, and participants were able to reflect on, refine, and relate their views to their faith and experience.

"We had a really good discussion on relationships and marriage."

"One person expressed a traditional view of marriage. The next week, they said they had been thinking all week and now believed that gay people shouldn't be denied marriage."

It opened up the opportunity to have pastoral conversations which we wouldn't have been able to have."

Figure 11: Levels of agreement with statements about deeper understanding.

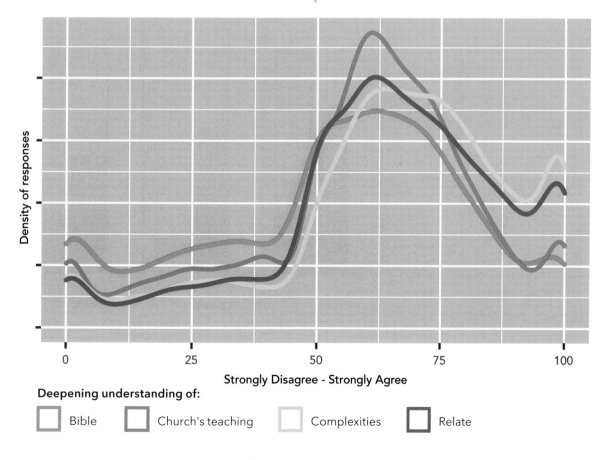

Density of responses

Strongly Disagree - Strongly Agree

Deepening understanding of:

☐ Bible ☐ Church's teaching ☐ Complexities ☐ Relate

"A friend of mine was in a group and had never heard of things like 'transsexual', so it was all new to him. He really had to go home and process all of this."

66

I thought I knew exactly where I stood but it was good to be exposed to other ideas."

Another way that the LLF Course encouraged participants to engage with deeper learning was by pointing to further resources available on the LLF Hub. *Figure 12* shows the ways in which the various LLF resources were used by the participants. The story films were the most popular resource, followed by the LLF Book.

Only 24% of course leaders used the "Going further" resources more than occasionally.

Figure 12: Use of LLF resources other than the course.

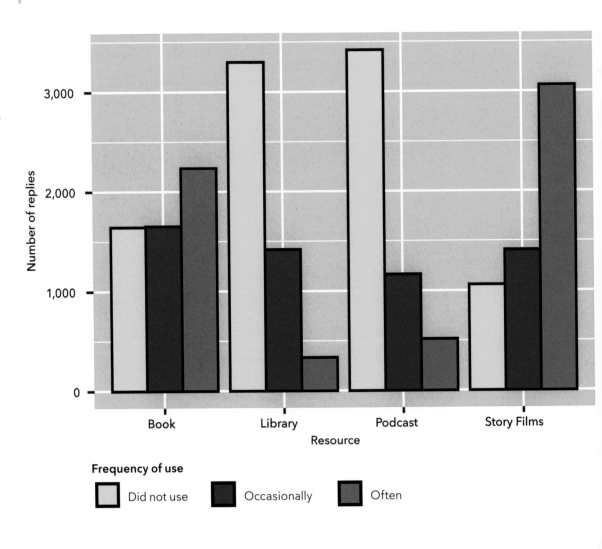

What did participants learn?

The question 'How has engaging with this course made a difference for you?' prompted responses that reflect a number of themes. Each of these is described in turn.

Increased awareness of diversity and LGBTQ+ experience

One of the most popular responses to the questions about what difference the course has made, or might make, was that engaging with the course had increased awareness and understanding. Respondents wrote about increased awareness of LGBTQ+ experience, including the rejection some have faced in church.

"I hope that the real-life stories and the invitation to reflect will show people who are unaware that LGBTI Christians belong to the church and have just as rich a faith as any other Christians. I hope that the stories will make people aware of how badly LGBTI Christians are being treated by the church in general and how much we are suffering because of it and that positive change will result locally, including more LGBTI people experiencing the fulness of God's love."

Some people commented that their eyes were opened to contemporary discussions about sexuality and gender diversity, and that their knowledge of previously unfamiliar subjects – such as sexual diversity and trans experience – had increased. Several described the course as "enlightening".

66

...I felt I had had my eyes opened to the world around me in 2021."

"I hope that it will make our congregation more aware of issues of gender and identity and help them to be more open minded."

"Make people realise it's an issue that's important to talk about."

"We felt that the overall experience of the course was insightful and helped us to gain a greater understanding of the complexities surrounding the topics of same-sex marriage and same-sex activity."

Depth, clarity, confidence

Participants said that the LLF Course helped to "clarify" their thoughts and point of view.

> "It has helped to clarify some of the issues."

> "It has prompted me to revisit previous articles and booklets I have read, and to think more deeply, trying to go beyond my preconceptions."

> "It has strengthened my own views on these issues; but it has also reminded me of the complexity of the issues involved."

Some found that the course enabled them to feel more confident in articulating their thoughts and engaging discussion about the subject.

"

I am now more confident to express my beliefs about sexuality, diversity and inclusion."

> "It has given me the confidence to approach discussions on the content within a framework of CofE application of scripture."

> "Helped with a vocabulary for these conversations."

> "More confident in raising topics of gender and sexuality with other Christians."

Compassion

As well as encountering new information and clarifying knowledge, some responses spoke of engaging emotionally with the subjects of LLF. Participants reflected on increased feelings of empathy and compassion for LGBTQ+ people, including new awareness of the "hurt" experienced.

> "It hasn't changed my orthodox convictions, but I hope that I have more compassionate understanding of those who do not."

> "I have more empathy but am still confused about my views."

> "It has made me realize the pain that not accepting people from the LGBT community is causing."

Confirmed views, new attitudes

Some course participants had their initial views confirmed:

> "More aware of some of the issues. Interestingly enough, more affirmed in my own, in many respects, traditional understanding of these."

> "It has strengthened my belief in the love of God for all whatever their gender."

"Now confident that my views on human sexuality agree with this course and has reinforced my sympathy with gay people."

Moreover, some found that the course galvanised them to act on their stance.

"It has challenged me to push for change and to stand up for those who have made different life choices."

"It has strengthened my resolve to work for change in the Church of England."

"Made me more determined to broaden my congregation's experience of biblical hermeneutics and alternative theological interpretations of the Bible."

Almost no one cited a wholesale change in their opinion or stance on the topics covered by LLF. However, some did describe a change in attitude or approach:

66

It made me look again at my views and prejudices."

"It has helped me to be open minded and understand how others feel."

"Made me more liberal in my views."

66

It makes me realise that the subject is no longer something I can think doesn't affect me."

Several of the survey respondents spoke of increased "openness", including being more "open minded", being more open with fellow church members, open to "different interpretations of the Bible", more open to "engage with others" on these topics, openness to "accepting difference".

Some told us that they left the course feeling confused, conflicted or uncertain as they did not reach a desired resolution:

"I still have a sort of cognitive dissonance to what the Bible says and what I'd prefer it to say or not say."

"I remain very conflicted. I have read widely around this over several years and the arguments and scriptural interpretations are persuasive in both directions. What my heart and mind say don't always match and I am fearful of doing harm. I am left feeling as though I need to read, pray and think a lot more."

A poem

As a salmon swimming upstream to spawn,
With mighty effort against the flow,
Hope despite experience.
I journey on, navigating leaps, rapids, rocks
With fierce determination.

Caviar of narrative needs to be deposited
In some still, imagined pool
of receptivity,
Left to develop and grow,
Nurtured by Nature and listening.

Over five weeks I transition from
buoyant saltwater
To vapid so-called fresh.
An uncomfortable environment
Where I and mine are examined, discussed,
speculated upon
By grizzly bears with raking claws.

I choose not to identify publicly as fish
In this liminal space between bank and river,
Do not desire predators' attention.
I have no wish to be dissected
by those biblical teeth
And hide instead behind rocks and shadows.

There are rules of engagement;
A Geneva convention of pastoral principles
Along battlelines of principled positions.
You in your small corner, I in mine
Engaging in combat as well as exploration.

To be fair, you did not know that
I was one of the 'them'
That you segregated from your own species.
I heard how it was OK to be me
so long as I was celibate.
I heard that justice meant obedience,
Liberation meant release from this
particular personhood.

My hermeneutics differ;
Perhaps due to scales and tail.
Can fur, feather and fin speak
the same language?
I wanted it to be so.
But hear this, whatever your tongue.

When I reach the end of my climb
Depositing my eggs in a final gesture.
You must believe
It will not be the spawn of Satan.

*A poem written in response
to engaging with LLF.*

What aspects of learning generated most discussion?

The LLF resources set out to help people encounter the experiences of people who would otherwise have been invisible to them. They also hoped that taking part in LLF would enable participants to learn about 'different ways of reading scripture together well – exerting its transforming and revelatory power.' The responses in this section reflect whether – or to what degree – these hopes have been met.

Stories

Almost three-quarters of the leaders (73%) reported that the story films had generated most discussion, followed by the Bible study (45%) and learning together (40%).

The story films received particularly high praise across several of the survey questions. People appreciated having "real life" examples to think with and discuss. Similarly, for almost all the focus group participants the true stories were the most memorable and influential part of the course. They were seen to reveal the experience of others in a powerful way.

Three personal stories were particularly mentioned: the young man who identified as same sex attracted and was choosing to be celibate, the two women in a relationship who were very active in their church, and the married couple where one partner is transgender. Some people saw these as positive and some as negative stories, but most regarded them as compelling.

> "Coming from a not very diverse church it was hugely beneficial to engage with the personal stories presented."

> *For me, the stories brought things to life, a real eye opener to see the breadth and diversity of Christians and their lived experiences."*

> "Great to hear stories. Lifts it from the pages into lived experience."

> "I was moved by my own reaction, but also other reactions in the group."

> "It was a surprise and refreshing to use the videos."

> "Your heart went out to those people who are rejected from parts of the church."

> "There was a lot of pain and rejection in the stories, and it really stuck with me."

"The most surprising thing was to see people who were rejected in churches - I had never been aware of this - to see that people get such negativity when they come to church, to imagine it is not a safe place was quite shocking. For a person like me who has always been to church, I have never been uncomfortable."

"The videos were very powerful. I watched them all through and the fact they ended with "we're living in love and faith" was very affirming."

"It is such an honour to hear those stories."

Use of the Bible

Alongside the personal stories, the use of the Bible in the LLF Course was one of the most discussed topics in the focus groups. There were strong views expressed by many participants that important parts of Scripture were not included or not handled appropriately.

"The Bible was not treated as the main authority."

"There was not enough biblical content so that we could get under the text."

"I feel like the course could have engaged more directly with some of the 'difficult' passages of scripture. At times it felt like we went out of the way to avoid discussing these even though our group were keen to!"

A response created while taking part in a focus group.

> *"*
>
> *I felt the course was rather light in exploring Biblical passages and examining possible alternative interpretations of these."*

Participants came to different understandings of marriage and sexuality from the Bible. Some felt that there was a deliberate attempt to not present what some might refer to as a 'traditional biblical view', particularly about the institution of marriage.

> "Are people reinventing what is said in the Bible?"

> "Even in LLF it says the Bible says there is no other way than man-woman relationship, so is the Church confused?"

> "Stick to what the Bible says: marriage is between a man and a woman."

> "There was no one coming forward who gave the biblical view. There is sin and we need to be more aware of that, and the wrath and judgement of God, as it says in Scripture."

Many others argued for a different understanding where the biblical approach is less traditional regarding the institution of marriage and/or LGBTQ+ equality:

> "My plea is that the biblical view of marriage changes all over the Bible. I'm nervous of people who just pick verses – to allow apartheid, allow slavery, stop those who died by suicide to be buried in hallowed ground. The Bible is so important, but it is so complex; there is no one view of marriage in the Bible at all."

> "God made me. I didn't choose to be the way I am. With the Bible, it is all to do with interpretation and translation. It is about love."

Bible and stories

A number of focus group participants saw a tension between engaging with the Bible and people's stories. There was concern about the relationship between biblical authority and lived experience. These sentiments were also reflected in the questionnaire responses: some respondents were concerned that there was not enough close biblical engagement. It was suggested that the course relied on "emotion" rather than starting from Scripture.

> "There was an over-emphasis on story rather than biblical discussion, which meant the group couldn't have an honest discussion."

> "It was distressing to see personal stories seen as equivalent to Scripture."

"We talked about feelings a lot but not a lot about Scripture and didn't come back to Scripture in the end."

"What really came to me most strongly is the fundamental differences in what we believe the Bible tells us, and we need to bring that out into the open and talk to each other."

Many in the focus groups concluded that the question of how we approach the Bible is at the heart of different convictions.

"I didn't like how the Scriptures were used. It would have been interesting to hear how and why people used the Scriptures in different ways."

66

This is bigger than sexuality, it is really about the Bible."

66

I think tackling how we understand how we read the Bible is a more helpful way to open the doors … we need the Holy Spirit to open and speak through the texts."

A prayer written in response to engaging with LLF.

Love, sex, marriage, friendship

God where are you in all of this?

"Be in the world but not of the world."

Thinking about this theologically is challenging.

Quick to express compassion and understanding but

I struggle to see how everyone's story can be "right"

Lord Jesus Christ help your church to hear your voice

Lead us in paths of righteousness even if that's difficult for us

For you are the One who understands all of this!

Make me a Channel of your peace

I want to be peaceful. I want to keep learning. I want to be happy. This is made difficult by the offensive statement on p.25 of the course booklet as follows:

Identity in Christ

How does all this relate to our discussion of identity as followers of Christ? This is not a task that falls only on LGBTI+ people. It's a task for all of us. As Christians, we agree that our deepest identity is in Christ and that we all need to take sin and the need for transformation seriously. We agree that all humans are equally loved by God and we rejoice in our diversity. We may not agree, though, about human experiences in the areas of gender and sexuality. Are they part of the God-given diversity of humans created in God's image? Or are they marks of the brokenness of that created image which God is working to restore?

This statement allows for there to never be on acceptance of all people, regardless of their orientation and suggests God would agree !!!

Never stop LEARNING!

happy ending
L₁ O₁ V₄ E₁

A response created while taking part in a focus group with the following commentary: "Feeling apprehensive. Churns your stomach. Rise of emotion. Not sure what that's about... An article from the Church Times... then I got another CT article... Never Stop Learning. The middle of the image is from p.25 of the [course] book that I found very offensive. There are good things about the course but... We may not agree... Marks of brokenness... to restore. The quote from p. 25 negates the whole thing for me... this paragraph made it quite difficult. To have something undermine... offensive and disappointing... A sense of being hurt by the course."

How did participants learn?

People learn in different ways. The LLF resources tried to be accessible to the diverse ways in which people learn. The responses in this section reflect how participants felt about learning together about subjects that are personal and about which there is disagreement.

A new kind of learning ... and leadership

For many people in the focus groups, the topics discussed and the process of the LLF Course provided a new kind of learning. The way the course was run, with an emphasis on listening and open discussion, was considered an innovative and valuable development.

> "It seems to me that the value of this exercise is the process as well as the outcome .... create more courses like this on pressing issues using a similar structure."

For some participants it was the first time that the topics had been discussed in their church.

> **"**
> *It was good to discuss things that have never been discussed before."*

> "A lot of people said the church has never talked about sex, or marriage, or [being] LGBTQ+ before, but now we can, as a first step."

> "The congregation has had little exposure to those with different sexualities before."

A consequence of this new kind of learning was that the leader/facilitator was found to influence respondents' experience of the course. Most questionnaire responses on this were positive:

> "Our facilitator understood the content well and presented it in a gentle patient and non-judgemental way."

> "Our facilitator was excellent and made sure it was a safe environment, meaning that participants felt able to express their views."

A few found their facilitators were too forthcoming with their own views or too "controlling" of the discussion.

> "The course was good, however it was heavily influenced by the leader (Vicar) and his views on the subject which he was very clear about, not wanting to listen to anything other than his view."

> "The course was sometimes led from the front and ideas pushed on us which I did not like."

A response created while taking part in a focus group, with an accompanying comment: "The three lines are the Trinity. The buildings are the organised church. Kind deeds… what I've experienced. The challenge of this course to an educated liberal is: on what ground does my conviction stand? On what ground, does my Christianity and faith stand? How do you relate to scripture? How do you know which bits of Bible are negotiable and ignorable? … it feels as though it can slither through your fingers… I now have a problem with scripture that I had not had before."

A 'word cloud' created from a group in Rochester Diocese after engaging with LLF.

Living in Love and Faith feedback

Diocese of Rochester
called together

According to some focus group participants, group facilitators that guided the discussion to allow all viewpoints created a better experience for those involved. It is noted that much of this was explicitly informed by the use of the Pastoral Principles in practice.

"

There was a light bulb meeting when someone said, "I am so relieved we are talking about this", and then from then on everyone felt able to talk honestly, openly, and compassionately and relax with each other."

"We managed to accommodate somehow with those who have very different views and not leave anyone behind, and to journey together."

"The Pastoral Principles are such an important background. It moved us on as a church with all sorts of issues. We were able to approach each other with love and understanding which was great."

According to other participants, some facilitators were less proficient which meant that meaningful discussion was limited.

"There was a bit too much emphasis on getting through the material, as there was so much of it, rather than finding the space to discuss and explore."

"I don't think the facilitators prepared for it enough."

How was learning shared?

Learning and gaining new insights often prompt people to share this with others. It can be a measure of the significance and relevance of the learning that has taken place.

That is why participants were asked how they had shared their learning with others. *Figure 13* shows that the vast majority (86%) had shared their learning in some way, mainly with friends, at church (68%), and outside church (50%). People also wrote that they had shared it with family members (5%), workplace colleagues, or (other) clergy and church staff.

Figure 13:
How learning
has been
shared.

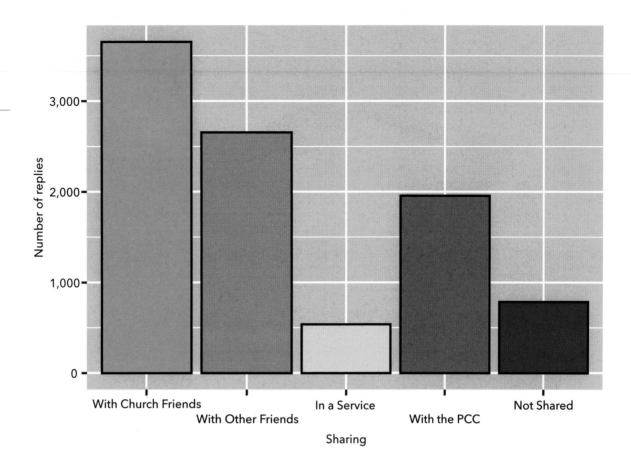

Image (right):
A response
created while
taking part in a
focus group.

Image (left):
A response
created while
taking part in a
focus group.

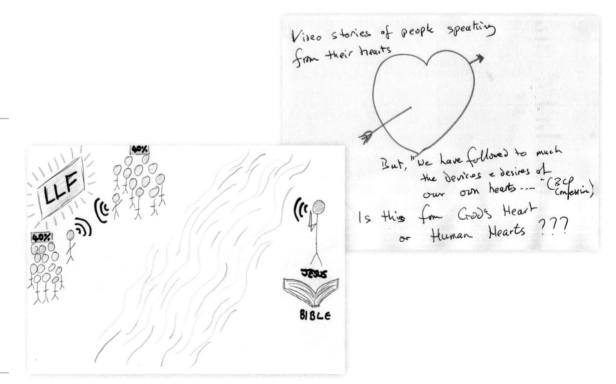

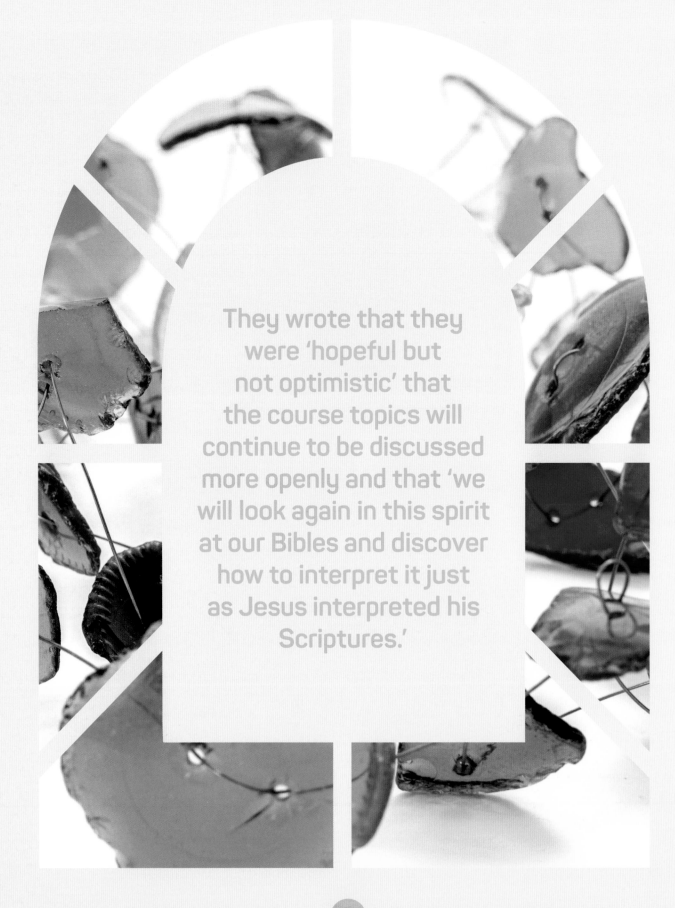

They wrote that they were 'hopeful but not optimistic' that the course topics will continue to be discussed more openly and that 'we will look again in this spirit at our Bibles and discover how to interpret it just as Jesus interpreted his Scriptures.'

A story about

learning to reconcile holiness and compassion

A course participant in their 'ninth decade' submitted a response summarising their learning.

They wrote: *'God's ways are not our ways'* before noting that *'however much I think I am right in my understanding of the Bible and LLF topics'*, the course brought to light the *'many graduations in such understanding'* within church that *'we frequently gloss over'*. This includes those who have taught *'from the front'* over the last 20 years. *'We have assumed a uniformity of view which is rarely defined or discussed.'*

They described the concept of *'identity'* as being *'new to me, perhaps because I don't use social media much and watch quite a narrow range of TV'*. Despite being a difficult concept, they appreciated the opportunity to learn. They felt the course had been important for defining the word *'marriage'* more precisely, compared with other types of partnership. They also felt it was important to understand what *'authority of Scripture'* meant, and wished that the course had dealt with Bible passages on gender, sex or marriage in a more direct way.

In response to the question *'How has this course affected your life and that of my church?'*, they noted, *'It is impossible and much too soon to say. It left me quite anxious and confused.'* They wrote that they were *'hopeful but not optimistic'* that the course topics will continue to be discussed more openly and that *'we will look again in this spirit at our Bibles and discover how to interpret it just as Jesus interpreted his Scriptures.'*

The participant was hopeful but not optimistic that a way will be found to reconcile the Bible's 'clear, disturbing morality and calls to holiness' with 'Jesus' love and compassion for the lost and outcast'.

Relating

Joining in conversations

Many of the survey respondents told us that the LLF Course has started a conversation:

It has been a start where there has previously been relative silence."

"There were no startling new insights, but it was good to be prompted to discuss matters with which I have wrestled, often privately, for many years."

"It's good to feel it's not such a taboo subject within the church."

"It was a helpful start to potentially difficult but necessary conversations on sexuality and gender in the church."

Discussions were "illuminating" and a highlight of the course experience for many course participants:

"I loved the fact our Church was embracing this course and willing to engage in very frank conversation about all issues raised. Amazingly we had a mix of people and we all respected each other's views."

"Most helpful was engaging with fellow church members discussing the subject and their views and insights."

"Discussions were at times very challenging. They led to much reflection between sessions. It was also enlightening to learn other's views and to share my own."

> ❝
>
> *Deep and meaningful discussions resulted. People shared things that they had not before."*

Of those who were critical of the course content, many were still pleased with the opportunity to discuss these subjects:

"Fortunately, we didn't let the course material get in the way of a good discussion."

There is a desire to continue these conversations:

"I hope that those of us who took part will feel enabled to have conversations with others – acknowledging and valuing everyone, and being prepared to talk about diversity and loving relationships."

"It's a good starting block for further discussion and easier when it is generated from a Church of England source."

"I hope it will lead to open, informed and respectful discussion between people of all points of view."

Specifically, there is a desire to take the conversation to church members who have not yet taken the LLF Course. It is hoped that further conversations would cover more breadth as well as diving deeper than the course allowed:

> ❝
>
> *I think it is a brave start to the process but the conversations need to become more public and widespread."*

"I hope more people from local church will do this course and would like to see open and frank discussions within local church ahead of any potential scenarios occurring in real life."

Engaging with diversity and disagreement

Many respondents appreciated learning from diverse views and experiences in their groups and had positive experiences of disagreeing well with others:

"Was very good, people were respectful, some things were said that could be taken the wrong way however it was good to allow them to say what was needed and for a 'gay' perspective to be put on it as they hadn't thought about it in this way and said were naive. This was the same from me as a non-Christian gay married woman. I would much rather have an open and honest conversation than people turn around and say things behind my back."

To have such a mixed group was great as it provided a variety of life experiences and views."

While we couldn't always agree, we were able to disagree without acrimony and tried to understand others' views."

"It was good to see that we disagreed on certain things but that we agreed to disagree."

"It was a good experience of diverse views respectfully heard."

Some told us that they learned to better understand opposing points of view and became more tolerant of them.

"The course certainly enabled me to empathize with various viewpoints that much better."

"I have felt that I understand the points of view of others on the subjects better. I wonder how many felt inhibited to speak like I did."

It has enabled me to understand other Christians who are different to me."

In some cases, where participants represented a minority opinion in their group, there was reluctance to share. Some noted that group members were timid in their contributions "in case they upset anyone or offended them."

"Because most of us were of a more open and inclusive perspective, the one person who wasn't kept saying she didn't want to take up the time defending their position."

"I was worried my traditional views would cause problems."

> **"**
> *I was the only one in my group that expressed my particular view. I did manage to speak but it was an uncomfortable experience."*

In other cases, an outspoken minority was seen to deter others from contributing:

"One or two members expressed opinions that were opposed to the messages in the course. The majority seemed supportive, but I sensed a reluctance to speak out openly in support – perhaps because of not wanting to disturb an initiative that is long overdue."

"We had a couple of people out of the 12 who had very strong views which was a difficult dynamic to encounter, especially for the course leader."

"I felt that a few, with more extreme views, were allowed to dominate discussion and restrict exchange of opinions. The views were largely conservative."

"Aware of a minority who were very vocal in expressing their views, which may have hindered others from joining in."

A response created while taking part in a focus group.

the opposite of faith is not doubt but certainty

A response created while taking part in a focus group.

Many groups reported that they were like-minded and fairly "uniform".

"Interesting discussions but all the same view point."

"Good, we were not that varied in views and were all rather agreeable. I guess we are victims of our own echo chamber."

Like-minded groups expressed that they would have liked more diversity:

"Group had variety of experiences but I would say all were open and supportive of the issues – it would have been interesting to have some present who struggled with material more…but they didn't come to the course."

"There was a limited range of viewpoints in the group, so perhaps with some more variety, there may have been deeper and more informed discussions, pertaining to other viewpoints."

"While the group represented the congregation there was little variation in lived experience which meant we had to rely on the story videos etc. to understand other points of view."

"I would have liked to have had more variety in my group, we were all heterosexual, married with children."

Focus group participants who had experienced different groups in a variety of settings offered a view on how well the groups functioned. Groups with people drawn from a broader area or from different churches seemed to work better.

"I took part in a deanery group … I wanted to be challenged by other opinions."

"When it was done as a deanery it was far more successful … in listening together, learning together, and feeding back."

"I was disappointed in our parish group with how it didn't open minds."

"The parish one didn't work because we all knew each other too well and were guarded against each other. The deanery one was a meeting of personalities, minds, experiences, and backgrounds that didn't usually rub up against each other."

However, other respondents found that that the presence of differing opinions was challenging and led to friction in group discussions.

"Those at the extremes found it hardest to engage. There were 3 conservative evangelicals who all failed to finish the course and 2 LGBT Christians who told the whole group that they had suffered at the hands of conservative evangelicals in their small group discussions. Those 'in the middle' had a better sense of how they could facilitate the course locally."

"I felt judged by some for believing the traditional view of sex and marriage is the correct one. At times I was "grilled" by those who believe differently and forced to defend my beliefs."

Focus group participants commented on the personal and pastoral dynamics that need to be attended to in conversations like these:

> ❝
> *I found it very difficult not to take things personally, because it's my life and the way I live."*

"The hardest thing in being a facilitator was helping people to listen to each other."

"We need to make sure that we go out of our way to love the people who have been hurt, whatever our position."

Some focus group participants expressed frustration when disagreement didn't surface, for whatever reason:

"If people can't be authentic, we can't be an authentic church."

"I didn't want us to have disagreements, but I felt like I missed something by not disagreeing, if that makes sense."

"I'm willing to speak to people who want a genuine conversation, but the church isn't willing."

Being safe

The subject matter of LLF is deeply personal and impacts on people's lives, faith and identity. This is particularly true for LGBTQ+ people. In a different way, it impacts people who have made life decisions in accordance with convictions that are perceived to be out of touch with cultural norms. It was vital, therefore, to find out whether people felt safe as they engaged together in groups with the LLF Course.

The questionnaire asked LLF Course group participants how safe they felt in speaking in their group. Their responses are shown in *Figure 14*. Almost everyone felt very safe in speaking in their group, with the mean score 84 and the median, 91. On average, people who identified as heterosexual rated their safety within the group as 91 out of 100, while those that did not identify as heterosexual were just 1 point less, at 90, out of 100. The median value for people who described themselves as trans was 92, and for those who described themselves as cis was 91.

It's important to note that these are responses from people who have chosen to complete the feedback. Those who had a negative experience may be less likely to complete the questionnaire.

Figure 14: Safety in speaking in the group.

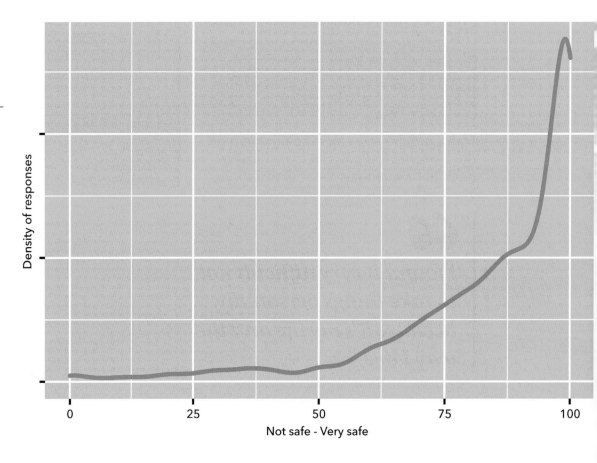

Density of responses

0   25   50   75   100

Not safe - Very safe

As has been hinted above, where people spoke of feeling reluctant to speak if their views were in the minority, people's feeling of safety may be related to the degree of diversity within the group. When these two aspects were considered together, there was, overall, no difference in feelings of safety in diverse or homogenous groups. The vast majority of responses are at the very safest end of the scale and spread out across all types of diversity.

Many questionnaire respondents reported feelings of safety and openness in their groups which made for good conversation.

"People felt totally free to express their views."

"Friendly, encouraging, supportive."

"There was a significant degree of openness and candour which was really helpful."

66

We felt confident enough to be honest to each other with our thoughts and feelings."

Some highlighted that initial shyness reduced as the course progressed. In other cases, this inhibition persisted. In the focus group discussions, participants reported that some participants felt safe, if not at the beginning, then certainly by the end. A number remarked how the Pastoral Principles helped participants to engage respectfully with each other.

"We all knew each other fairly well via church life but were shy to begin with, encouraged to speak by our leader. As each session progressed we became more open and shared our thoughts, feelings, and understanding."

"I have a female partner, and even though people in church are traditional they were very welcoming of me and my partner."

"There were people in my group with very different views, but the Pastoral Principles meant that no one got angry despite coming from very different approaches … we respected one another."

66

People were very careful in how they expressed their views and did so with love, but that's because they knew each other."

In the focus group discussions, participants said that for some the process did not feel safe, either for themselves or for others. Most people who did not feel safe in the LLF Course process were from the LGBTQ+ community. However, a minority of people who held conservative viewpoints also highlighted how there were points where they too didn't feel safe.

> 66
>
> *I felt very shut down as a gay person for the whole course ... somehow, I kept going ... it was a very painful process."*

"It was evident that LGBTQ+ people were asked to do a lot of stepping up ... it was the expectation that we would share our story ... as the powerless minority. You don't want to be constantly used like that and made to speak out."

"I am made to feel like I'm a homophobe or oppressive if I don't hold liberal views, made to feel like a monster and not loving, which is not true. I don't feel people who hold conversative opinions on the matter are respected any more."

> 66
>
> *Those with a traditional point of view felt silenced."*

"I don't think there was a lot of pastoral care embedded in the course – such a contentious topic, and the disagreements brought up a lot of past hurt and trauma."

"A lot of people feel they have listened but not been heard."

"It is funny how those who are most attuned to microaggressions and vocab are not in my experience very self-reflective of how they use language, because they think they have justice on their side."

Sacred Love

From generation to generation
landscapes change
humans evolve
God remains

Christians are called to glory
God, through voices and bodies

sexual beings, we are temples
of God's Holy Spirit

spirit beings, we are instruments
of Creator's grace

shaped for love
and intimacy
in different forms
we relate, in every aspect of our lives,
as God's beloved.

— Catherine Okoronkwo

The Marriage Pattern – A Song

Back there, in the garden,
It wasn't good to be alone
He made us for relationship
To know and to be known
So God designed a marriage
Reuniting man and wife
For faithfulness and fruitfulness
A home to nurture life

For this reason, a man shall leave
His father and his mother
and be united to his wife
And they shall become one flesh

The Lord and His people
Have been through ups and downs
They turned away, rejected him
Sought to steal his crown
They have been unfaithful
He is always true
Wooing them despite their sin
Loving them anew

One day there came a bridegroom
Who never took a bride
Who taught the marriage pattern
And what it signified
That just as man loves woman
And she delights in him
So Jesus loves his bride the church
And gave his life for them

We wait for Jesus' marriage
To the city that's above
With longings in our body
To remind us of his love
Some will marry sooner
Some will marry then
But all who are one with Jesus
Will know love that has no end

A song written and composed in response to engaging with LLF.

Use this QR code to listen to the song

This kneeler was created by Ros Clarke as part of telling her story in response to engaging with LLF.

A sculpture created in response to engaging with LLF, entitled, 'Imago Dei'.

The person who contributed this creative response explained that "this artwork was created by a dear friend in America. It is how he sees 'God' as neither male or female, but as a 'Divine Creator and a Universal Being'." [Courtesy of 'The Naked Pastor' available at https://nakedpastor.com/ Accessed 01 July 2022]

Finding connection

Some people told us that taking part in the course revealed to them the opinions of fellow churchgoers – perhaps also revealing the diversity of views within the church:

> "I understood the different view points within the Church better after the course."

> "Useful for people to learn about the range of perspectives in the Church both more widely and in our own church."

Others spoke of being disappointed or pleasantly surprised by the opinions of fellow church members:

> "Group discussions opened up my mind to how blinkered fellow Christians can be."

> "Sadly, it merely revealed the depth of the disagreements within the Church about not only sexuality but also other issues (e.g. Biblical authority)."

> "I was pleased to hear that we have an open church. I always thought it but have had it confirmed."

> "I was pleasantly surprised on how forward thinking many members were when I had wrongly made assumptions about their stance on same sex relationships for example."

Another theme in participants' feedback in the questionnaire was the increased feelings of connectedness within congregations and course cohorts as a result of taking part in LLF together. Some focus group participants felt that their church community was brought closer together through the learning process, even without complete agreement on the issues.

It was daunting to do but a very valuable experience that actually made us closer."

> "I believe I now know members of the church better."
> "I feel more connected to my church community."

> "I have met some lovely people we began as a group of strangers in week one and by week five we all felt like we were co-pilgrims affirming each other as we travelled together."

> "We had different views, but a level of trust built up. We were able to say what we felt in a way that was held by everyone in the group, whether we agreed with each other or not. Relationships between people grew."

"Our group was demographically similar but theologically diverse, but we managed to leave differences standing and live with the difference."

"I felt I was a bit more understanding of people who disagree with me. There's such importance in being able to value the people you don't agree with."

"We genuinely listened to each other … and tried to understand where they were coming from."

"We agreed to disagree. We did not go out to argue with each other. The conversations were tremendous and encouraging."

" "

As a parish we felt transformed by it, and we all learnt to listen better as the Body of Christ."

A sculpture created in response to engaging with LLF.

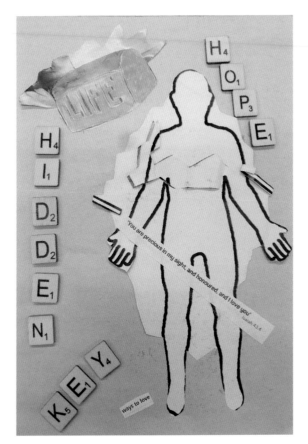 

A response created while taking part in a focus group, with an accompanying comment:
"An image with a zig zag section across the chest to pull back to reveal layered colours.
Although the course presented as being as equal in opportunity - the process is more costly
for LGBT+ people, things are hidden - the key hasn't really been opened.
A deeper consultation with people would've borne more fruit. Life and the spirit in hope -
there must be something in the process.
It was meant to be an equal line but I don't think it is.
Bible verse: 'You are precious in my sight and I love you.'"

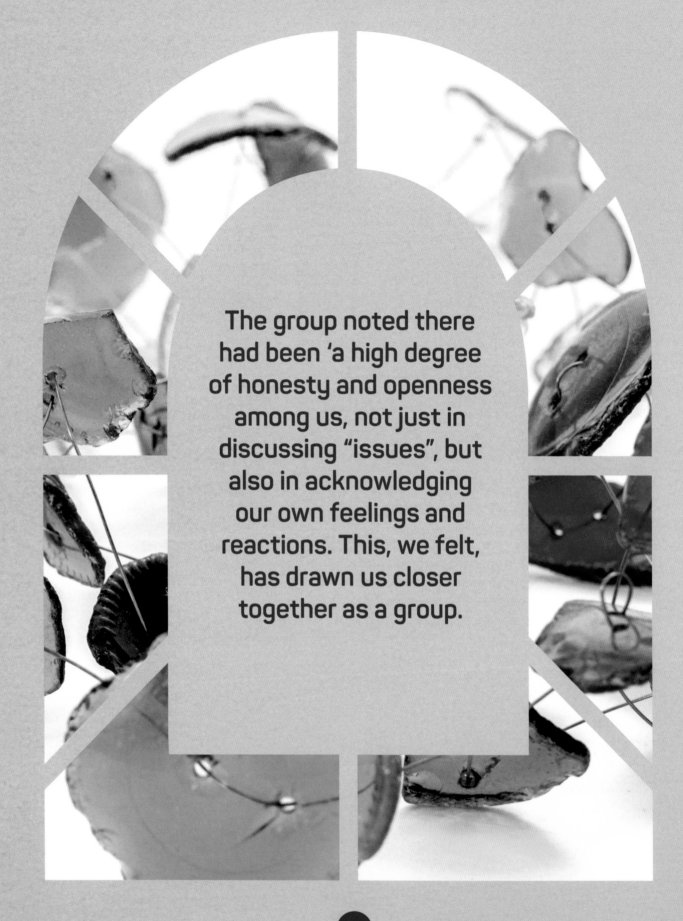

The group noted there had been 'a high degree of honesty and openness among us, not just in discussing "issues", but also in acknowledging our own feelings and reactions. This, we felt, has drawn us closer together as a group.

A story about

relating honestly in diversity and disagreement

One group's anonymous submission outlined their learning in a group of ten participants holding 'a range of perspectives'. This was an existing small group who devoted five meetings to look at course sessions and included a sixth follow-on session to reflect together on their 'thinking and feeling about the many difficult issues raised', which included some straw polling of opinion.

This group was described as being made up of some with strongly held traditional views that same-sex partnerships *'always fall short of God's plan for people's lives'*. Another saw no reason why the Church should not *'get on and catch up with where society is on this'*. Then there were several who weren't quite sure what to think, some of whom valued the *'strong traditional Christian influence'* they had grown up with but recognised that what they were previously taught *'may need re-evaluation if the Church is to be engaged with issues that society finds so important'*.

By the end of the course, all agreed LLF helped them to listen to the experiences of others by way of the *'short story films'* and all recognised that some people are same-sex attracted and some have *'a sense of unease about their gender, perceiving a mismatch between their biological sex and their gender identity'*.

The straw poll (conducted with care so no vote influenced another) confirmed the range of perspectives. On whether *'the Church of England should maintain its current doctrinal position'*: 2 agreed definitely, 2 were undecided/unsure, 1 disagreed on balance and 1 definitely disagreed.

The group noted there had been *'a high degree of honesty and openness among us, not just in discussing "issues", but also in acknowledging our own feelings and reactions. This, we felt, has drawn us closer together as a group'*.

Being Church

Welcome, inclusion, acceptance

The questionnaire responses show a widely held desire for the church to be welcoming to all. This desire for welcome is shared by those with otherwise diverse views. Some said that they hope for increased "acceptance" and others spoke in terms of "active inclusion".

> "That there will continue to be an attitude of generous welcoming."

> "I hope we are more welcoming to all people with whom we have contact. I also hope that we express our desire to remain faithful to God by sticking to the biblical pattern for marriage, sex and identity."

> "I want an inclusive, loving, faithful Church, that is diverse and loves Jesus."

> *I hope people will find a place of welcome even amongst differing views on sexuality."*

> "I hope that there will be an opening of the acceptance of difference that Jesus demands."

> *I hope the church finds a way to work together to find ways to show love and hospitality to everyone regardless."*

"I hope we will continue to be explicit and open about how inclusive we aim to be, and to check that this really is the message we give out."

"I hope that the national Church will accept the rich diversity of God's creation and recognise that God doesn't solely speak to us through scripture, but also through the cries of God's people who long for inclusion and dignity."

A response created while taking part in a focus group.

Some focus group participants spoke about the need for more welcome and inclusion more generally:

> *Single people can feel very isolated and excluded in church, especially with this increasing focus on family – that is married with children."*

> *There are a lot of ways people can be excluded in church and not welcomed, and not just sexuality. It could be language barriers, or class or whatever."*

Change

Several focus group participants shared the experience of being treated negatively in church and stated that the church needed to change its standpoint and how it treated people.

"People have faith in God but they're not keen on the institution – because of its lack of inclusiveness."

"Society has changed but the Church hasn't – gay people being forced to hide, not be their true self, not being their true self to God."

"Some people in our group said, 'love the sinner and not the sin.' Would you actually say that to their faces? It made me question whether it was appropriate for those people to be welcomers at our church."

> " The Holy Spirit has spoken, the nation has changed, social attitudes have changed, and the Church now needs to change."

"I didn't realise that churches could treat people so badly."

"I hope that the Church will change, but I am not sure that it will."

A response created while taking part in a focus group.

Sorry...Please

SORRY...
Sorry for all the discrimination and prejudice
Sorry God for not being consistent in prayers
Sorry for the LGBT+ people who are stigmatised in society
Sorry for being selfish
Lord, we are so sorry that some people feel excluded
Sorry for all the people we have excluded
Sorry for the discrimination in football, both racial and homophobic,
sorry the church does not support single sex marriages
Sorry for spreading hate and discrimination and not trying
to understand the LGBTQ+ community
Sorry for not being patient and understanding of people who are not educated
Sorry God for not always treating others as we would like to be treated
Sorry for the people that are judgemental and don't respect others
for their opinion, sorry for not being a great ally
Sorry for people spreading stigma about the LGBTQ+ and the
discrimination of people, please make the world a peaceful place

PLEASE...
Please make people more tolerant and understanding
Dear God, why are people full of hate?
Give us wisdom to make the right decision in these areas
which require thought, generosity and love
Thank you Lord that people are considering talking about issues
|of equality in society, may talks turn into action
Please help with guidance
Please help us to be more welcoming to all
Please make people more tolerant and make people more
understanding of the changing of the times
God please I am asking you for success in life and happiness in my family
Thankyou God for loving us all as precious sheep in your flock
Please move the church in the direction of inclusivity

*A prayer written in response
to engaging with LLF.*

Orthodoxy and tradition

A section of respondents expressed concerned that the course will "lead people astray from the Bible." Some spoke of their traditional "values [as] under threat".

> "I do hope that it reinforces the determination to follow the Bible and not be tempted to fit in with the world."

> "The CofE needs to be clear about what the Bible says, how to love all people, how we treat the LGBT community. We must not shy away from upsetting the LGBT community just because it makes our life easier."

> "I pray that it will lead to a recovery of confidence in the church's traditional understanding of these issues."

A minority of focus group participants stated that they did not want the church to avoid challenging people regarding LGBTQ+ equality even if this was painful or costly.

> *The church should be holy and walk in God's way. We must be caring and do outreach for all people to find Jesus."*

> "Love involves telling people hard things sometimes. We are called to live holy lives … not bringing from our culture into the Bible."

> "Welcoming and missional, listening to the Holy Spirit. God knows what is best for each person, but we shouldn't be compromised or change our minds … Jesus is the same yesterday, today and for ever."

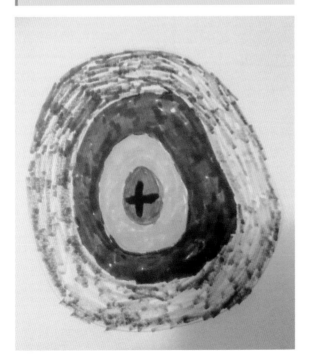

A response created while taking part in a focus group, with an accompanying comment: "My picture is of Jesus in the centre and rings around the outside of people in the Church and outside and how close they felt to Jesus by how the Church treated them. I hope that whatever happens Jesus is at the centre of it all."

Same-sex relationships and marriage

A persistent theme in the survey answers was same-sex marriage. Most of the comments on this theme expressed hope that the LLF Course might contribute to the "acceptance of same sex marriage" or "blessing of same sex partnerships". This came up in focus group discussions as well.

> "I hope the Church will make changes to its rules, especially by celebrating same-sex marriages and by allowing LGBTI+ priests and other ministers to live openly."

> "The national Church needs to allow same sex weddings but clergy whose beliefs won't allow this should not be forced to hold them or feel they have to leave the church."

> "I hope the CofE will learn that the silent majority are now in favour of extending both Liturgy and Canon to all consenting couples for marriage and blessing of faithful relationships"

> "I struggle with heterosexual people who want to get married in church but have no faith and no intention of going to church … but if you're LGBTQ+, even if you attend that church, have faith and are part of the community, you don't have the same welcome or love and you can't even receive a blessing."

> "The Church of England is much more closed and behind, and it needs to catch up. The Methodists have allowed equal marriage."

A smaller number presented the opposing view, speaking against such a change in doctrine:

> "That we will be able to hold loving grace-filled relationships whilst holding to an orthodox view of sexuality and marriage."

> "I hope it will lead to greater empathy and inclusion and that the sanctity of marriage between one man and one woman till death us do part will be upheld."

> "I hope that the national Church will make a firm resolution to confirm the present situation. I also hope that there will not be any change to the form of marriage or any blessing of same sex relationships or any watering down of responsibility so that individual ministers could agree to something in their church."

76

Understanding of God

The focus group conversations offered an opportunity for deeper reflection. Participants were asked if doing the LLF Course had changed their understanding of God. Perhaps an unexpected question for some, many needed time to think and reflect about their reply.

"It is really hard to put into words … I think it's broadened my understanding of God and of humanity, especially as what people were talking about is quite under the radar and not spoken about."

"In the course, God is taken as read and understood, which isn't the case at all. I think trying to define what God thinks says something rather important about how the course has been structured."

> **I wonder every night, God, what do you make of all this?"**

"In one of the videos, someone said that God wants them to be happy – I don't think God says that – rather God wants us to be a holy people."

"Thinking about the flesh of God – you can't separate the body from the soul, so sexuality and relationships are part of the body of God, of Christ."

"God is in the messiness and this course was too tidy."

"God is so much bigger than my own view."

"What it has made me realise is very simple – God is love, and we start from that perspective. That's my main signpost – the Church needs to include people who hold different views."

> **I have been prompted through the whole process to focus more on God's grace."**

Image (right): A response created while taking part in a focus group.

A story about
being church and the most important thing

The leader of a church youth group submitted a response about the group's engagement with the LLF Course. This group of 11–18 year olds knew each other and their leaders well: they had been meeting fortnightly for over four years.

The leader described the sessions as *'one of the most engaging series of themed studies we have embarked upon as a group […].The story films provided a way into the discussions and could be recalled in detail several weeks later. The group were frequently shocked by stories of individuals having being excluded, rejected or side-lined by a church when a particular relationship or sexuality had been disclosed, which has not been their experience in this church in which they have grown up, at school or at home'.*

The young people *'were well-versed with the language and definitions of sexuality and gender identity and had a good understanding of societal issues of inclusion, prejudice and abuse. Most had direct experience of knowing someone who was gay, lesbian, bisexual or transgender from school or, in two cases, in their own immediate family'.* Key themes that emerged from the group's discussions were equality, inclusion, justice and Christian love for all. The young people described a person's relationship with Jesus as *'the most defining feature of our identity as Christians'.*

When invited to write an open letter to the church in response to their learning, one young person wrote, *'please be welcoming and gentle to our new congregation and be respectful to anyone who has their own life path. Pray for their relationship with God and don't judge anyone by their gender / sexuality […] the most important thing in our lives is the relationships we and those around us have with God. Help us have humility, gentleness when it comes to other relationships that aren't our own'.*

Key themes that emerged from the group's discussions were equality, inclusion, justice and Christian love for all. The young people described a person's relationship with Jesus as 'the most defining feature of our identity as Christians'.

Moving forward

The significance of LLF

Participants emphasised the importance and relevance of LLF's subject matter:

> "It is an area that affects many aspects of our day to day life and is becoming increasingly important, we cannot rely on ignorance as an excuse."

> "Because it seems the Anglican Church could split on the matter of same sex marriage, and people should be informed about the issues and listen and have their say."

> "Because [LLF] addresses some of the key issues that provide barriers to us moving forward as a church."

> "Because [LLF] covers incredibly important areas that the church needs to focus on to be a light in the world."

Some highlighted that engagement with LLF was important for perceptions of the church, both in relation to churchgoers' understanding of the Church of England's stance, and to the way the Church is perceived by the wider public.

> "I think it would be good for people to be aware of the matters highlighted in the course, and hopefully to show that the national Church are trying to engage with modern life."

> "Think it is fundamental in encouraging non-believers to investigate Christianity."

Some expressed that if the Church of England fails to engage with issues of diversity and inclusivity, then younger generations will be put off joining or staying in the church.

"I also pray for those sections of society that find the church laughable and displaying hypocrisy for their efforts over this issue and the people who will not be drawn to Church/ Jesus because of the example set. I also pray for the youth of today who see judgments measured out by people wearing purple robes and see their friends and class mates (colleagues/ family) excluded from Church and therefore from Salvation. This particularly breaks my heart and I feel will cause the church to crumble as younger people will find it too difficult to work in an organisation that isn't able to accept changing society."

"I think the Church of England is in huge, huge trouble, if it does not start accepting LGBTQAI folk as equals. It is a violation of UK law. I am a younger adult than most churchgoers and can assure the CoE that if it does not start to be inclusive, most people my age will not tolerate it being in charge of schools, politics, or charities going forward. In twenty years' time people my age will be in charge, the majority of current churchgoers will be dead. A church vs state separation is most definitely coming if the church does not adapt on this. And, as I asked my mini group, I ask you the same question: Is this really the hill you want the CoE to die on?"

A response created while taking part in a focus group.

Church unity

Many questionnaire respondents hope that through LLF, church members will gain greater openness to others' views; that diversity of opinion in the church will be respectfully acknowledged; and that the church will be united.

> "I hope that we will learn to disagree gracefully, to allow for differences of opinion to be acknowledged and accepted, but to move on to becoming a more inclusive church, and to avoid the harm caused to many brothers and sisters in Christ who have been excluded or vilified."

> "Hopefully most people will come to accept that there is more than one valid point of view and see others as just as much valid Christians as they are."

> "I hope that we can agree to disagree in love."

> "My message would be the same – ONE VIEW for all the Church. We might not all agree with it, but you would know what is expected."

> ❝
> *I hope and pray that God uses LLF to keep the CofE together. Schism would be an offence to God and a hammer blow to our mission."*

Most focus group participants thought that the unity of the Church is paramount, and church leaders need to work to preserve this.

> ❝
> *Jesus cries out for unity – but we have to figure out how."*

> "Christ calls us to unity – we shouldn't have to split as a church. What is the Holy Spirit saying to the Church today? It is time for us to listen."

> "None of the content of LLF is heretical. It's real people, real relationships. We need to hold each other in the process."

> "The Church needs to develop the skills of speaking to each other, listening, reconciling, engaging and mediating. We need a truth and reconciliation project."

> "Do you want a more united Church than at present? – if so, look at the most caring, respectful pathway."

> ❝
> *We can't all agree, but we can accommodate our differences."*

However, some suggested that LLF might lead to division in the church. Some were clear that proclaiming the truth is more important than preserving the unity of the Church.

"The national church is the 'largest ecumenical' experiment ever to be conceived and therefore we should expect and welcome a diverse response to LLF. We will all be changed by the course and the next steps. Some will stay where they are but others will find a fresh impetus to kingdom building."

"Having regard to the depth of the disagreements, it is hard to say. Perhaps it will help everyone to recognise the roots of these disagreements but I don't see it resolving them."

"I hope it doesn't lead to gay marriage being sanctioned. I believe a move like this would divide the church."

"Is unity ever an attainable goal?"

"There is part of me that sometimes wonders if there is a need for some sort of break for the truth and reconciliation to happen. Perhaps a break would facilitate listening and conversation."

"Pursue what is true without trying to hold something together that I don't think can hold together in its current form."

"We have to disagree with love, despite our differences."

"If we have to split, we have to split. Give us places to go."

"Give us the freedom to express different views and different ways of living."

"I fear that the bishops want to make same sex marriages legal. I wonder how many people will leave the Church if they do this, and if nothing happens, how many other people will leave?"

"I pray that change will happen soon – even if it means schism."

Unity that is paper thin is not really unity."

A painting created in response to engaging with LLF entitled, 'Cross of Transformation'.

The Church of England

While the course led some to feel encouraged and hopeful about the Church of England's position…

> ## *It has encouraged me that the church is trying to catch up with the rest of society in recognising that humankind is diverse."*

"I feel more positive about the church's future."

"Given me hope."

"It has given me hope that we may yet hold together as a church despite our differences as long as we all refrain from drawing lines in the sand."

…many felt that LLF saw the Church of England avoiding making a clear statement on matters of sexual and gender diversity – attempting to "have its cake and eat it", or simply "kick the issue into the long grass". Some expressed frustration and disappointment about the Church's direction.

"It has made me feel even more dispirited about the Church of England's seriousness of intent in engaging with issues relating to sexuality, identity and relationships."

"Made me even more aware that I am not sure where the Church of England is going."

"I feel less hopeful for the Church of England."

"Just reinforced my anxiety that the Church of England wants to stray from the clear Christian teaching and accommodate the latest trends."

> ## *Making me feel even more strongly that the Church has lost its direction."*

A painting created in response to engaging with LLF entitled, 'What next?'

NOW WHAT?

For some respondents the course furthered their impatience for the Church to act and galvanised them to bring about change.

"It has made me even more passionate about campaigning for equal marriage."

"It's also made me more determined to work for change towards a more inclusive Church of England."

"Engaging with this course has reinforced my view that the church cannot continue inflicting pain and suffering on LGBTI Christians in the way that it is currently (and has done historically) and that this is a matter for urgent attention rather than leisurely discussion."

Respondents expressed that they want Church leaders to listen to congregations:

"I would hope that the national Church would be listening to the messages being sent by this church-wide initiative and draw up policies accordingly."

"Hopefully the hierarchy will actually listen to what parishes/parishioners are saying and not to 'what their itching ears want to hear'."

"I hope that the process will show the national Church leadership what the range of views is amongst clergy and laity; that it will act as something akin to a 'citizens' assembly' to guide future decision-making in this area."

A response created while taking part in a focus group.

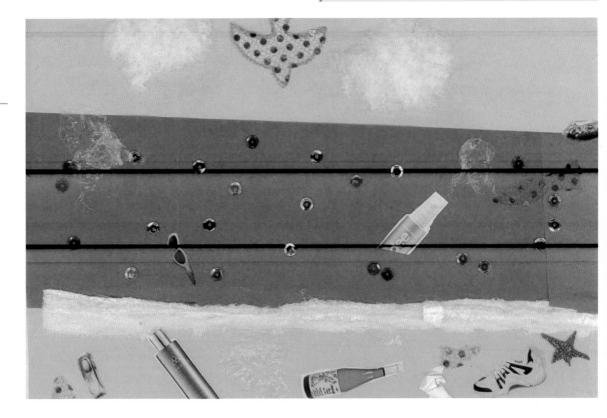

Making decisions

The question of how the Church should make decisions was a topic of conversation in some focus groups. Most, but not all, accepted that the episcopate should lead the approach of moving forward in love and faith.

"The bishops should be leading us towards doctrine and sound faith. LLF is investing a lot of time in bottom-up and not top-down, and this isn't episcopal."

"We need [bishops] to give us that theological specialism of what is a human being, from a theological perspective that is creedal, that is about the incarnation, redemption and the cross."

"We need the bishops to use their apostolic witness."

"The bishops have an authority given to them. It is not democracy … it is up to us to accept the bishops' decision, hopefully highly informed."

"The bishops have a responsibility to counter and banish all erroneous doctrine."

"It is good that we were doing this and making an effort to find out where people are at and what the range of opinion is, rather than impose a top-down solution."

"Look to the lay leadership to progress some of this, as they are not so trapped by hierarchy."

"I am a bit worried that at the end of the whole LLF process we'll throw it back to the "grown-ups" (the bishops) to squabble all over it again."

"The shepherds need to know what we, the sheep, are actually saying."

Image (right): A response created while taking part in a focus group.

Hope

Fear

Dear bishops,

Be bold, brave and true

Participants in focus groups were asked what message they would pass on to the bishops, and the majority of respondents understood that, overall, the House of Bishops have a difficult but essential task, and that a decision on moving forward needs to be made soon.

Most people in the focus groups suggested that the decisions made by the House of Bishops needed to be bold, courageous, clear and honest. While some advocated strongly for change and some to maintain the Church's position on questions of sexuality, all agreed that coming to a clear decision soon is vital.

Image (right): A response created while taking part in a focus group.

"Please be brave and tackle it. We need to deal with it and be bold and decisive. My generation and below won't be attracted to the Church if it doesn't move on this."

"If we don't get over this it will be a missiological disaster that will go on and on."

"Don't make it wishy-washy; whatever decision you make, it needs to be clear and meaningful."

"Please be honest and say what you believe, because doing one thing and saying another doesn't help."

"Think carefully, what is the heart of Jesus and what is Scripturally right."

"All of this in the backdrop of Covid, climate change and the war in Ukraine – there are much bigger things going on at the moment."

"I think in the global Anglican Communion there are massive global issues going on, and we should not squabble and split over this."

"The decision time has come; the nation is watching."

Some had further messages they wanted to relay to the bishops.

"You are representing everybody, so I guess it's very difficult."

"I don't want you to think you have listened to everyone because you haven't."

"We need to pray for you as this may be the hardest thing you will ever have to do."

"You need to seriously listen."

"Have you all done the course, and if not, why not?"

"I need you to be people of prayer, Scripture, sacraments, and the Communion of Saints."

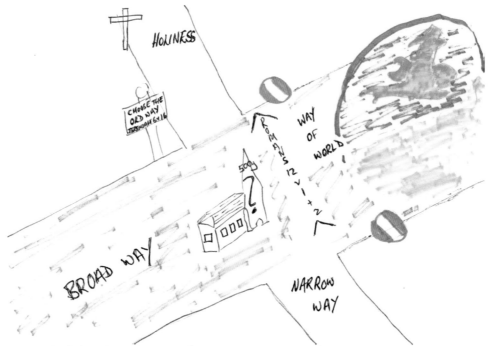

A response created while taking part in a focus group with the following commentary: "The Church of England has been upholding the Truth of God's word for nearly 500 years, but it seems to find itself at a crossroads. It is as if newer thinking of the last 50 years or so somehow makes the teaching of scripture from Genesis to Revelation outdated, no longer culturally relevant (even though LLF acknowledges that the Bible never commends other than male and female marriage). I have called it the narrow way and the broad way. There are scriptural cautions in Jeremiah to choose the old ways and in Romans to be touched by the mercies of God and do not let the world squeeze you into its mould. I do beg the Archbishops and Bishops to let themselves be touched by the mercies of God and the tenets of scripture rather than the attractive and fashionable ways of the world. The Bible has never been a democracy. It is the Word of the Living God."

A prayer from the closet

Broken One, whose body is given
to being transfigured, to signalling
beyond performance and appearance,
I want to lose and find myself
in the reflection in your eyes.

Spirit, you search all that is left unsaid
and unrealised. Help me see whether
some treasures are best left
beneath the soil, safe from the corrosive air.

How can clothes and jewellery
meet the task of laying bare the soul?
Still, you taught me not to say 'just symbols',
for what have we to bind ourselves together
except for ritual?

Christ, I am scared of our people—
terror, not of hatred, but of promises to love us
in spite of who we are (or might become);
tolerance and pity would only shatter me
more quietly than violence.

Still, maybe one day I will take the risk
of letting my body assume
a truer shape than this. But, for now,
I will go into my room,
and close the door,

and offer praise for all these strange revelations
you are kindling in me.

*A prayer written in response
to engaging with LLF.*

A story about
moving forward honouring faithfulness and commitment

One member of the clergy wrote to 'put on record a number of proposals about the constructive steps which might be taken' to 'embrace the "radical Christian inclusion"' hoped for through the LLF learning process.

They expressed concern that Issues in Human Sexuality was *'no longer fit for purpose in expressing the mind of the Church'*. As a study document, it was never *'approved'* as the Church's teaching by General Synod and Synod members had recently *'invited the House of Bishops to reflect on the fact that it alludes positively to forms of conversion therapy for bisexual people'* which is not *'consonant with General Synod's express decision to reject conversion therapy'*.

Issues in Human Sexuality (1991) was *'drafted before the development of civil partnerships and equal marriage'* and *'casuistical interpretations of this text … have not served to create healthy and open discussions around sexuality and ministry'*. In their view, *'it has generated a culture of fear and anxiety for LGBTQ+ clergy and lay ministers. We need to create greater honesty and openness around issues of relationships, loneliness, trust and integrity in ministry. We also need to remember that prurience has never been a Christian value.'*

> **'We need to create greater honesty and openness around issues of relationships, loneliness, trust and integrity in ministry'.**

They went on to write they believed in equal marriage not because they were *'a liberal'* but because they *'believe that faithfulness and commitment matter'*. On the assumption that developments towards equal marriage might *'proceed in the same vein'* as the *'gentle, if untidy, pastoral pragmaticism'* adopted to address divorce and remarriage in the Church, they suggested two things. First, *'a revised liturgy for the Dedication of a Civil Marriage'* should be developed to recognise *'that Civil Marriage means equal marriage'*. Second, conscience clauses should be introduced for ministers and parishes *'who might object to equal marriage'*.

A story about
moving forward with confidence and compassion

A PCC offered feedback in the form of statements of belief. They began by acknowledging the pastoral challenge of discussing these matters which is 'painful and difficult' for many 'of all shades of opinion' in the Church of England and the Anglican Communion.

Their response addressed the question of same-sex marriage assuming this was why the LLF materials had been produced. They believed the Church's *current doctrinal position reflects biblical teaching*'. The church should not change its position '*or adopt policies or practices that are inconsistent with it*': same-sex marriage and the blessing of same-sex relationships should not be adopted.

They believed the Bible's teaching is also clear about abstinence outside marriage for those in opposite-sex relationships. However, the church's emphasis '*on families comprising of a married couple and children*', has had negative effects '*resulting in those who are single feeling excluded*'. They also expressed concern that '*an overemphasis on sexual relations*' has inhibited the '*development of strong and deep non-sexual relationships including between people of the same sex, which are valued in the Bible*'.

They outlined the need for repentance, the struggle with sin and dealing with the consequence of sin for everyone, without exception. The church is made up of sinners so there is '*no ground for*

any Christian to reject another' and '*we should seek to help one another in our struggles*' by showing '*forgiveness, love and sensitivity*', growing in our following of Jesus, obeying God's commands.

This church was also concerned about questions of gender. They believed that '*the Bible indicates that humans are created as either male or female*' and '*the concept of gender fluidity is not in accordance with its teaching*'. Yet pastoral sensitivity is needed for those affected by this due to the pain experienced in gender dysphoria. They were especially concerned for young people and believed the church should speak out against the dangers of young people '*taking decisions that could impact the rest of their lives*'.

The church's emphasis 'on families comprising of a married couple and children', has had negative effects 'resulting in those who are single feeling excluded'.

92

Conclusion

Gratitude and hope

At the beginning of the engagement stage of the LLF journey, the Next Steps Group articulated their shared hopes for the LLF journey.

Participation
We hope that there will have been the widest possible participation across the whole Church.

We hope that we will have engaged in deep learning together about God and about being human.

Outcome
We hope that everyone can see that they have been listened to, heard, loved, and taken seriously.

We hope that the Spirit's work among us has resulted in a revelation of something new, unexpected.

Relationships
We hope that we will have learned to be kinder, understanding one another's perspectives better.

We hope that we will have become more at ease with ourselves as a Church.

The Future
We hope that our deeper understanding and love will enable us to face new questions in a better way.

We hope to remain hopeful as we move into the future together in love and faith.

Thank you to all who, daring to hope, travelled together on this journey.

What does it mean to live in love and faith, to move into the future together in love and faith?

Even to ask the question involves exercising hope. Not wishful thinking, but the certain hope that, as people of God, we are commanded to embody and embrace.

It is a hope that 'does not disappoint us, because God's love has been poured into our hearts through the Holy Spirit that has been given to us.' (Romans 5.5)

Acknowledgements

The following individuals and organisations were responsible for different aspects of the work described in this publication:

Brendan Research
Fiona Tweedie, Emma Teale and Claire Dalpra designed, managed and analysed the LLF questionnaire and analysed the independent submissions.

Church Army's Research Unit
John Tomlinson and Lu Skerratt designed, organised and facilitated the focus groups, analysed the conversations, and curated the creative contributions that were made during the focus groups.

ASD Arts and Education
Simon Davies designed and managed the LLF Hub and managed the creative contributions that were submitted through the LLF Hub.

Alice Walker, David Ferrier and Matt Eaton created the 'Faith and Fracture' sculpture and soundscape that was on display in York Minster.

Alice Walker, David Ferrier and Simon Davies curated the creative contributions into a multimedia art installation that was exhibited at General Synod in July 2022 and at the first of the College of Bishops' gatherings in September 2022.

The Next Steps Group is immensely grateful for the painstaking work undertaken by these individuals who have handled every response with such care to make sure that what is presented holds a mirror to what the many people who participated wanted to convey. This report is the outcome of their spirit of teamworking and unstinting commitment to the vision and aims of Living in Love and Faith.

Church House Publishing
Church House
Great Smith Street
London SW1P 3AZ
www.chpublishing.co.uk

Commissioned by the Living in Love and Faith Next Steps Group
of the House of Bishops of the Church of England

Published for the Living in Love and Faith Next Steps Group
by Church House Publishing 2022

ISBN 978 0 7151 1198 7

British Library Cataloguing in Publication Data
A catalogue record for this book is available from the British Library

Designed by Narrative Design
Printed in the UK by Core Publications Limited